RUM TASTING

LOGBOOK

THIS BELONGS TO

PHONE	EMAIL
START DATE	LAST DATE

CONTENTS

CONTENTS

RUM LOG

RUM NAME		DATE TASTED

PRODUCER	DISTILLERY

TYPE / GRADE	COUNTRY OF ORIGIN

STILL TYPE	REGION

AGE	ALCOHOL %	PRICE	BOTTLE SIZE

QUALITY RATING

1	2	3	4	5	6	7	8	9	10

VALUE FOR MONEY

1	2	3	4	5	6	7	8	9	10

COLOR METER

- BLACK
- DARK BROWN
- MAHOGANY
- BRICK
- DARK AMBER
- AMBER
- GOLD
- STRAW
- CLEAR

FLAVOR WHEEL

HEAT / ABM _____ %

BALANCE
FINISH
BODY
PEATY / SMOKY
SHARP / ACIDIC
ASTRINGENT
ROASTED / WOODY
MOLASSES
SWEET / CANDIED
SPICES
HERBAL / VEGETAL
DRIED FRUIT
CITRUS FRUIT
DARK FRUIT
FRESH FRUIT

FLAVOR NOTES

SMELL / SCENT NOTES

OTHER NOTES

RUM NAME		DATE TASTED

PRODUCER	DISTILLERY

TYPE / GRADE	COUNTRY OF ORIGIN

STILL TYPE	REGION

AGE	ALCOHOL %	PRICE	BOTTLE SIZE

QUALITY RATING

1	2	3	4	5	6	7	8	9	10

VALUE FOR MONEY

1	2	3	4	5	6	7	8	9	10

COLOR METER

- BLACK
- DARK BROWN
- MAHOGANY
- BRICK
- DARK AMBER
- AMBER
- GOLD
- STRAW
- CLEAR

FLAVOR WHEEL

HEAT / ABM _____ %

BALANCE
FINISH
BODY
PEATY / SMOKY
SHARP / ACIDIC
ASTRINGENT
ROASTED / WOODY
MOLASSES
SWEET / CANDIED
SPICES
HERBAL / VEGETAL
DRIED FRUIT
CITRUS FRUIT
DARK FRUIT
FRESH FRUIT

FLAVOR NOTES

SMELL / SCENT NOTES

OTHER NOTES

RUM LOG

RUM NAME		DATE TASTED

PRODUCER	DISTILLERY

TYPE / GRADE	COUNTRY OF ORIGIN

STILL TYPE	REGION

AGE	ALCOHOL %	PRICE	BOTTLE SIZE

QUALITY RATING

1	2	3	4	5	6	7	8	9	10

VALUE FOR MONEY

1	2	3	4	5	6	7	8	9	10

COLOR METER

BLACK
DARK BROWN
MAHOGANY
BRICK
DARK AMBER
AMBER
GOLD
STRAW
CLEAR

FLAVOR WHEEL

HEAT / ABM _____ %

BALANCE
FINISH
BODY
PEATY / SMOKY
SHARP / ACIDIC
ASTRINGENT
ROASTED / WOODY
MOLASSES
SWEET / CANDIED
SPICES
HERBAL / VEGETAL
DRIED FRUIT
CITRUS FRUIT
DARK FRUIT
FRESH FRUIT

FLAVOR NOTES

SMELL / SCENT NOTES

OTHER NOTES

RUM NAME	DATE TASTED

PRODUCER	DISTILLERY

TYPE / GRADE	COUNTRY OF ORIGIN

STILL TYPE	REGION

AGE	ALCOHOL %	PRICE	BOTTLE SIZE

QUALITY RATING

1	2	3	4	5	6	7	8	9	10

VALUE FOR MONEY

1	2	3	4	5	6	7	8	9	10

COLOR METER

BLACK
DARK BROWN
MAHOGANY
BRICK
DARK AMBER
AMBER
GOLD
STRAW
CLEAR

FLAVOR WHEEL

BALANCE
FINISH
BODY
PEATY / SMOKY
SHARP / ACIDIC
ASTRINGENT
ROASTED / WOODY
MOLASSES
SWEET / CANDIED
SPICES
HERBAL / VEGETAL
DRIED FRUIT
CITRUS FRUIT
DARK FRUIT
FRESH FRUIT
HEAT / ABM _____ %

FLAVOR NOTES

SMELL / SCENT NOTES	OTHER NOTES

RUM LOG

RUM NAME		DATE TASTED

PRODUCER	DISTILLERY

TYPE / GRADE	COUNTRY OF ORIGIN

STILL TYPE	REGION

AGE	ALCOHOL %	PRICE	BOTTLE SIZE

QUALITY RATING

1	2	3	4	5	6	7	8	9	10

VALUE FOR MONEY

1	2	3	4	5	6	7	8	9	10

COLOR METER

- BLACK
- DARK BROWN
- MAHOGANY
- BRICK
- DARK AMBER
- AMBER
- GOLD
- STRAW
- CLEAR

FLAVOR WHEEL

HEAT / ABM _____ %

BALANCE
FINISH
FRESH FRUIT
BODY
DARK FRUIT
PEATY / SMOKY
CITRUS FRUIT
SHARP / ACIDIC
DRIED FRUIT
ASTRINGENT
ROASTED / WOODY
HERBAL / VEGETAL
MOLASSES
SPICES
SWEET / CANDIED

FLAVOR NOTES

SMELL / SCENT NOTES

OTHER NOTES

RUM NAME	DATE TASTED

PRODUCER	DISTILLERY

TYPE / GRADE	COUNTRY OF ORIGIN

STILL TYPE	REGION

AGE	ALCOHOL %	PRICE	BOTTLE SIZE

QUALITY RATING

1	2	3	4	5	6	7	8	9	10

VALUE FOR MONEY

1	2	3	4	5	6	7	8	9	10

COLOR METER

BLACK

DARK BROWN

MAHOGANY

BRICK

DARK AMBER

AMBER

GOLD

STRAW

CLEAR

FLAVOR WHEEL

BALANCE   HEAT / ABM _____ %

FINISH

FRESH FRUIT

BODY

PEATY / SMOKY

DARK FRUIT

SHARP / ACIDIC

CITRUS FRUIT

ASTRINGENT

DRIED FRUIT

ROASTED / WOODY

HERBAL / VEGETAL

MOLASSES

SPICES

SWEET / CANDIED

FLAVOR NOTES

SMELL / SCENT NOTES

OTHER NOTES

RUM LOG

RUM NAME	DATE TASTED

PRODUCER	DISTILLERY

TYPE / GRADE	COUNTRY OF ORIGIN

STILL TYPE	REGION

AGE	ALCOHOL %	PRICE	BOTTLE SIZE

QUALITY RATING

1	2	3	4	5	6	7	8	9	10

VALUE FOR MONEY

1	2	3	4	5	6	7	8	9	10

COLOR METER

- BLACK
- DARK BROWN
- MAHOGANY
- BRICK
- DARK AMBER
- AMBER
- GOLD
- STRAW
- CLEAR

FLAVOR WHEEL

BALANCE · HEAT / ABM _____ %
FINISH · FRESH FRUIT
BODY · DARK FRUIT
PEATY / SMOKY · CITRUS FRUIT
SHARP / ACIDIC · DRIED FRUIT
ASTRINGENT · HERBAL / VEGETAL
ROASTED / WOODY · SPICES
MOLASSES · SWEET / CANDIED

FLAVOR NOTES

SMELL / SCENT NOTES

OTHER NOTES

RUM NAME		DATE TASTED

PRODUCER	DISTILLERY

TYPE / GRADE	COUNTRY OF ORIGIN

STILL TYPE	REGION

AGE	ALCOHOL %	PRICE	BOTTLE SIZE

QUALITY RATING

1	2	3	4	5	6	7	8	9	10

VALUE FOR MONEY

1	2	3	4	5	6	7	8	9	10

COLOR METER

BLACK

DARK BROWN

MAHOGANY

BRICK

DARK AMBER

AMBER

GOLD

STRAW

CLEAR

FLAVOR WHEEL

BALANCE

HEAT / ABM _____ %

FINISH

FRESH FRUIT

BODY

PEATY / SMOKY

DARK FRUIT

SHARP / ACIDIC

CITRUS FRUIT

ASTRINGENT

DRIED FRUIT

ROASTED / WOODY

HERBAL / VEGETAL

MOLASSES

SPICES

SWEET / CANDIED

FLAVOR NOTES

SMELL / SCENT NOTES

OTHER NOTES

RUM LOG

RUM NAME	DATE TASTED

PRODUCER	DISTILLERY

TYPE / GRADE	COUNTRY OF ORIGIN

STILL TYPE	REGION

AGE	ALCOHOL %	PRICE	BOTTLE SIZE

QUALITY RATING

1	2	3	4	5	6	7	8	9	10

VALUE FOR MONEY

1	2	3	4	5	6	7	8	9	10

COLOR METER

- BLACK
- DARK BROWN
- MAHOGANY
- BRICK
- DARK AMBER
- AMBER
- GOLD
- STRAW
- CLEAR

FLAVOR WHEEL

HEAT / ABM _____ %

BALANCE
FINISH
BODY
PEATY / SMOKY
SHARP / ACIDIC
ASTRINGENT
ROASTED / WOODY
MOLASSES
SWEET / CANDIED
SPICES
HERBAL / VEGETAL
DRIED FRUIT
CITRUS FRUIT
DARK FRUIT
FRESH FRUIT

FLAVOR NOTES

SMELL / SCENT NOTES

OTHER NOTES

RUM NAME		DATE TASTED

PRODUCER	DISTILLERY

TYPE / GRADE	COUNTRY OF ORIGIN

STILL TYPE	REGION

AGE	ALCOHOL %	PRICE	BOTTLE SIZE

QUALITY RATING

1	2	3	4	5	6	7	8	9	10

VALUE FOR MONEY

1	2	3	4	5	6	7	8	9	10

COLOR METER

BLACK

DARK BROWN

MAHOGANY

BRICK

DARK AMBER

AMBER

GOLD

STRAW

CLEAR

FLAVOR WHEEL

HEAT / ABM _____ %

BALANCE
FINISH
FRESH FRUIT
BODY
DARK FRUIT
PEATY / SMOKY
CITRUS FRUIT
SHARP / ACIDIC
DRIED FRUIT
ASTRINGENT
HERBAL / VEGETAL
ROASTED / WOODY
SPICES
MOLASSES
SWEET / CANDIED

FLAVOR NOTES

SMELL / SCENT NOTES	OTHER NOTES

RUM LOG

RUM NAME	DATE TASTED

PRODUCER	DISTILLERY

TYPE / GRADE	COUNTRY OF ORIGIN

STILL TYPE	REGION

AGE	ALCOHOL %	PRICE	BOTTLE SIZE

QUALITY RATING

1	2	3	4	5	6	7	8	9	10

VALUE FOR MONEY

1	2	3	4	5	6	7	8	9	10

COLOR METER

- BLACK
- DARK BROWN
- MAHOGANY
- BRICK
- DARK AMBER
- AMBER
- GOLD
- STRAW
- CLEAR

FLAVOR WHEEL

HEAT / ABM _____ %

BALANCE
FINISH
BODY
PEATY / SMOKY
SHARP / ACIDIC
ASTRINGENT
ROASTED / WOODY
MOLASSES
SWEET / CANDIED
SPICES
HERBAL / VEGETAL
DRIED FRUIT
CITRUS FRUIT
DARK FRUIT
FRESH FRUIT

FLAVOR NOTES

SMELL / SCENT NOTES

OTHER NOTES

RUM NAME

DATE TASTED

PRODUCER

DISTILLERY

TYPE / GRADE

COUNTRY OF ORIGIN

STILL TYPE

REGION

AGE

ALCOHOL %

PRICE

BOTTLE SIZE

QUALITY RATING

1	2	3	4	5	6	7	8	9	10

VALUE FOR MONEY

1	2	3	4	5	6	7	8	9	10

COLOR METER

- BLACK
- DARK BROWN
- MAHOGANY
- BRICK
- DARK AMBER
- AMBER
- GOLD
- STRAW
- CLEAR

FLAVOR WHEEL

HEAT / ABM _____ %

BALANCE
FINISH
BODY
PEATY / SMOKY
SHARP / ACIDIC
ASTRINGENT
ROASTED / WOODY
MOLASSES
SWEET / CANDIED
SPICES
HERBAL / VEGETAL
DRIED FRUIT
CITRUS FRUIT
DARK FRUIT
FRESH FRUIT

FLAVOR NOTES

SMELL / SCENT NOTES

OTHER NOTES

RUM LOG

RUM NAME	DATE TASTED

PRODUCER	DISTILLERY

TYPE / GRADE	COUNTRY OF ORIGIN

STILL TYPE	REGION

AGE	ALCOHOL %	PRICE	BOTTLE SIZE

QUALITY RATING

1	2	3	4	5	6	7	8	9	10

VALUE FOR MONEY

1	2	3	4	5	6	7	8	9	10

COLOR METER

- BLACK
- DARK BROWN
- MAHOGANY
- BRICK
- DARK AMBER
- AMBER
- GOLD
- STRAW
- CLEAR

FLAVOR WHEEL

BALANCE, HEAT / ABM _____ %, FINISH, FRESH FRUIT, BODY, PEATY / SMOKY, DARK FRUIT, SHARP / ACIDIC, CITRUS FRUIT, ASTRINGENT, DRIED FRUIT, ROASTED / WOODY, HERBAL / VEGETAL, MOLASSES, SWEET / CANDIED, SPICES

FLAVOR NOTES

SMELL / SCENT NOTES

OTHER NOTES

RUM NAME		DATE TASTED

PRODUCER	DISTILLERY

TYPE / GRADE	COUNTRY OF ORIGIN

STILL TYPE	REGION

AGE	ALCOHOL %	PRICE	BOTTLE SIZE

QUALITY RATING

1	2	3	4	5	6	7	8	9	10

VALUE FOR MONEY

1	2	3	4	5	6	7	8	9	10

COLOR METER

- BLACK
- DARK BROWN
- MAHOGANY
- BRICK
- DARK AMBER
- AMBER
- GOLD
- STRAW
- CLEAR

FLAVOR WHEEL

HEAT / ABM _____ %

BALANCE, FINISH, BODY, PEATY / SMOKY, SHARP / ACIDIC, ASTRINGENT, ROASTED / WOODY, MOLASSES, SWEET / CANDIED, SPICES, HERBAL / VEGETAL, DRIED FRUIT, CITRUS FRUIT, DARK FRUIT, FRESH FRUIT

FLAVOR NOTES

SMELL / SCENT NOTES

OTHER NOTES

RUM NAME	DATE TASTED

PRODUCER	DISTILLERY

TYPE / GRADE	COUNTRY OF ORIGIN

STILL TYPE	REGION

AGE	ALCOHOL %	PRICE	BOTTLE SIZE

QUALITY RATING

1	2	3	4	5	6	7	8	9	10

VALUE FOR MONEY

1	2	3	4	5	6	7	8	9	10

COLOR METER

- BLACK
- DARK BROWN
- MAHOGANY
- BRICK
- DARK AMBER
- AMBER
- GOLD
- STRAW
- CLEAR

FLAVOR WHEEL

HEAT / ABM _____ %

BALANCE
FINISH
BODY
PEATY / SMOKY
SHARP / ACIDIC
ASTRINGENT
ROASTED / WOODY
MOLASSES
SWEET / CANDIED
SPICES
HERBAL / VEGETAL
DRIED FRUIT
CITRUS FRUIT
DARK FRUIT
FRESH FRUIT

FLAVOR NOTES

SMELL / SCENT NOTES

OTHER NOTES

RUM NAME		DATE TASTED

PRODUCER	DISTILLERY

TYPE / GRADE	COUNTRY OF ORIGIN

STILL TYPE	REGION

AGE	ALCOHOL %	PRICE	BOTTLE SIZE

QUALITY RATING

1	2	3	4	5	6	7	8	9	10

VALUE FOR MONEY

1	2	3	4	5	6	7	8	9	10

COLOR METER

BLACK
DARK BROWN
MAHOGANY
BRICK
DARK AMBER
AMBER
GOLD
STRAW
CLEAR

FLAVOR WHEEL

HEAT / ABM _____ %

BALANCE, FINISH, BODY, PEATY / SMOKY, SHARP / ACIDIC, ASTRINGENT, ROASTED / WOODY, MOLASSES, SWEET / CANDIED, SPICES, HERBAL / VEGETAL, DRIED FRUIT, CITRUS FRUIT, DARK FRUIT, FRESH FRUIT

FLAVOR NOTES

SMELL / SCENT NOTES

OTHER NOTES

RUM LOG

RUM NAME	DATE TASTED

PRODUCER	DISTILLERY

TYPE / GRADE	COUNTRY OF ORIGIN

STILL TYPE	REGION

AGE	ALCOHOL %	PRICE	BOTTLE SIZE

QUALITY RATING

1	2	3	4	5	6	7	8	9	10

VALUE FOR MONEY

1	2	3	4	5	6	7	8	9	10

COLOR METER

- BLACK
- DARK BROWN
- MAHOGANY
- BRICK
- DARK AMBER
- AMBER
- GOLD
- STRAW
- CLEAR

FLAVOR WHEEL

HEAT / ABM _____ %

BALANCE, FINISH, BODY, PEATY / SMOKY, SHARP / ACIDIC, ASTRINGENT, ROASTED / WOODY, MOLASSES, SWEET / CANDIED, SPICES, HERBAL / VEGETAL, DRIED FRUIT, CITRUS FRUIT, DARK FRUIT, FRESH FRUIT

FLAVOR NOTES

SMELL / SCENT NOTES

OTHER NOTES

RUM NAME									DATE TASTED

PRODUCER	DISTILLERY

TYPE / GRADE	COUNTRY OF ORIGIN

STILL TYPE	REGION

AGE	ALCOHOL %	PRICE	BOTTLE SIZE

QUALITY RATING

1	2	3	4	5	6	7	8	9	10

VALUE FOR MONEY

1	2	3	4	5	6	7	8	9	10

COLOR METER

BLACK
DARK BROWN
MAHOGANY
BRICK
DARK AMBER
AMBER
GOLD
STRAW
CLEAR

FLAVOR WHEEL

BALANCE, HEAT / ABM _____ %, FINISH, FRESH FRUIT, BODY, DARK FRUIT, PEATY / SMOKY, CITRUS FRUIT, SHARP / ACIDIC, DRIED FRUIT, ASTRINGENT, HERBAL / VEGETAL, ROASTED / WOODY, SPICES, MOLASSES, SWEET / CANDIED

FLAVOR NOTES

SMELL / SCENT NOTES

OTHER NOTES

21

RUM NAME	DATE TASTED

PRODUCER	DISTILLERY

TYPE / GRADE	COUNTRY OF ORIGIN

STILL TYPE	REGION

AGE	ALCOHOL %	PRICE	BOTTLE SIZE

QUALITY RATING

1	2	3	4	5	6	7	8	9	10

VALUE FOR MONEY

1	2	3	4	5	6	7	8	9	10

COLOR METER

- BLACK
- DARK BROWN
- MAHOGANY
- BRICK
- DARK AMBER
- AMBER
- GOLD
- STRAW
- CLEAR

FLAVOR WHEEL

HEAT / ABM _____ %

BALANCE, FINISH, BODY, PEATY / SMOKY, SHARP / ACIDIC, ASTRINGENT, ROASTED / WOODY, MOLASSES, SWEET / CANDIED, SPICES, HERBAL / VEGETAL, DRIED FRUIT, CITRUS FRUIT, DARK FRUIT, FRESH FRUIT

FLAVOR NOTES

SMELL / SCENT NOTES

OTHER NOTES

RUM NAME		DATE TASTED

PRODUCER	DISTILLERY

TYPE / GRADE	COUNTRY OF ORIGIN

STILL TYPE	REGION

AGE	ALCOHOL %	PRICE	BOTTLE SIZE

QUALITY RATING

1	2	3	4	5	6	7	8	9	10

VALUE FOR MONEY

1	2	3	4	5	6	7	8	9	10

COLOR METER

BLACK
DARK BROWN
MAHOGANY
BRICK
DARK AMBER
AMBER
GOLD
STRAW
CLEAR

FLAVOR WHEEL

HEAT / ABM _____ %
BALANCE
FINISH
BODY
PEATY / SMOKY
SHARP / ACIDIC
ASTRINGENT
ROASTED / WOODY
MOLASSES
SWEET / CANDIED
SPICES
HERBAL / VEGETAL
DRIED FRUIT
CITRUS FRUIT
DARK FRUIT
FRESH FRUIT

FLAVOR NOTES

SMELL / SCENT NOTES

OTHER NOTES

RUM LOG

RUM NAME		DATE TASTED
PRODUCER	**DISTILLERY**	
TYPE / GRADE	**COUNTRY OF ORIGIN**	
STILL TYPE	**REGION**	

AGE	ALCOHOL %	PRICE	BOTTLE SIZE

QUALITY RATING

1	2	3	4	5	6	7	8	9	10

VALUE FOR MONEY

1	2	3	4	5	6	7	8	9	10

COLOR METER

- BLACK
- DARK BROWN
- MAHOGANY
- BRICK
- DARK AMBER
- AMBER
- GOLD
- STRAW
- CLEAR

FLAVOR WHEEL

BALANCE — HEAT / ABM _____ %

FINISH, BODY, PEATY / SMOKY, SHARP / ACIDIC, ASTRINGENT, ROASTED / WOODY, MOLASSES, SWEET / CANDIED, SPICES, HERBAL / VEGETAL, DRIED FRUIT, CITRUS FRUIT, DARK FRUIT, FRESH FRUIT

FLAVOR NOTES

SMELL / SCENT NOTES

OTHER NOTES

24

RUM NAME		DATE TASTED

PRODUCER	DISTILLERY

TYPE / GRADE	COUNTRY OF ORIGIN

STILL TYPE	REGION

AGE	ALCOHOL %	PRICE	BOTTLE SIZE

QUALITY RATING

1	2	3	4	5	6	7	8	9	10

VALUE FOR MONEY

1	2	3	4	5	6	7	8	9	10

COLOR METER

- BLACK
- DARK BROWN
- MAHOGANY
- BRICK
- DARK AMBER
- AMBER
- GOLD
- STRAW
- CLEAR

FLAVOR WHEEL

HEAT / ABM _____ %

BALANCE
FINISH
BODY
PEATY / SMOKY
SHARP / ACIDIC
ASTRINGENT
ROASTED / WOODY
MOLASSES
SWEET / CANDIED
SPICES
HERBAL / VEGETAL
DRIED FRUIT
CITRUS FRUIT
DARK FRUIT
FRESH FRUIT

FLAVOR NOTES

SMELL / SCENT NOTES

OTHER NOTES

RUM LOG

RUM NAME	DATE TASTED

PRODUCER	DISTILLERY

TYPE / GRADE	COUNTRY OF ORIGIN

STILL TYPE	REGION

AGE	ALCOHOL %	PRICE	BOTTLE SIZE

QUALITY RATING

1	2	3	4	5	6	7	8	9	10

VALUE FOR MONEY

1	2	3	4	5	6	7	8	9	10

COLOR METER

- BLACK
- DARK BROWN
- MAHOGANY
- BRICK
- DARK AMBER
- AMBER
- GOLD
- STRAW
- CLEAR

FLAVOR WHEEL

HEAT / ABM _____ %

BALANCE, FINISH, BODY, PEATY / SMOKY, SHARP / ACIDIC, ASTRINGENT, ROASTED / WOODY, MOLASSES, SWEET / CANDIED, SPICES, HERBAL / VEGETAL, DRIED FRUIT, CITRUS FRUIT, DARK FRUIT, FRESH FRUIT

FLAVOR NOTES

SMELL / SCENT NOTES

OTHER NOTES

RUM LOG

RUM NAME		DATE TASTED
PRODUCER	DISTILLERY	
TYPE / GRADE	COUNTRY OF ORIGIN	
STILL TYPE	REGION	

AGE	ALCOHOL %	PRICE	BOTTLE SIZE

QUALITY RATING

1	2	3	4	5	6	7	8	9	10

VALUE FOR MONEY

1	2	3	4	5	6	7	8	9	10

COLOR METER

BLACK
DARK BROWN
MAHOGANY
BRICK
DARK AMBER
AMBER
GOLD
STRAW
CLEAR

FLAVOR WHEEL

BALANCE, HEAT / ABM ____ %, FINISH, FRESH FRUIT, BODY, PEATY / SMOKY, DARK FRUIT, SHARP / ACIDIC, CITRUS FRUIT, ASTRINGENT, DRIED FRUIT, ROASTED / WOODY, HERBAL / VEGETAL, MOLASSES, SPICES, SWEET / CANDIED

FLAVOR NOTES

SMELL / SCENT NOTES

OTHER NOTES

RUM LOG

RUM NAME	DATE TASTED

PRODUCER	DISTILLERY

TYPE / GRADE	COUNTRY OF ORIGIN

STILL TYPE	REGION

AGE	ALCOHOL %	PRICE	BOTTLE SIZE

QUALITY RATING

1	2	3	4	5	6	7	8	9	10

VALUE FOR MONEY

1	2	3	4	5	6	7	8	9	10

COLOR METER	FLAVOR WHEEL	FLAVOR NOTES

COLOR METER

- BLACK
- DARK BROWN
- MAHOGANY
- BRICK
- DARK AMBER
- AMBER
- GOLD
- STRAW
- CLEAR

FLAVOR WHEEL

BALANCE · HEAT / ABM ____ %
FINISH · FRESH FRUIT
BODY · DARK FRUIT
PEATY / SMOKY · CITRUS FRUIT
SHARP / ACIDIC · DRIED FRUIT
ASTRINGENT · HERBAL / VEGETAL
ROASTED / WOODY · SPICES
MOLASSES · SWEET / CANDIED

SMELL / SCENT NOTES	OTHER NOTES

RUM NAME		DATE TASTED

PRODUCER	DISTILLERY

TYPE / GRADE	COUNTRY OF ORIGIN

STILL TYPE	REGION

AGE	ALCOHOL %	PRICE	BOTTLE SIZE

QUALITY RATING

1	2	3	4	5	6	7	8	9	10

VALUE FOR MONEY

1	2	3	4	5	6	7	8	9	10

COLOR METER

BLACK
DARK BROWN
MAHOGANY
BRICK
DARK AMBER
AMBER
GOLD
STRAW
CLEAR

FLAVOR WHEEL

BALANCE, FINISH, BODY, PEATY / SMOKY, SHARP / ACIDIC, ASTRINGENT, ROASTED / WOODY, MOLASSES, SWEET / CANDIED, SPICES, HERBAL / VEGETAL, DRIED FRUIT, CITRUS FRUIT, DARK FRUIT, FRESH FRUIT, HEAT / ABM _____ %

FLAVOR NOTES

SMELL / SCENT NOTES

OTHER NOTES

RUM LOG

RUM NAME		DATE TASTED

PRODUCER	DISTILLERY

TYPE / GRADE	COUNTRY OF ORIGIN

STILL TYPE	REGION

AGE	ALCOHOL %	PRICE	BOTTLE SIZE

QUALITY RATING

1	2	3	4	5	6	7	8	9	10

VALUE FOR MONEY

1	2	3	4	5	6	7	8	9	10

COLOR METER

- BLACK
- DARK BROWN
- MAHOGANY
- BRICK
- DARK AMBER
- AMBER
- GOLD
- STRAW
- CLEAR

FLAVOR WHEEL

HEAT / ABM _____ %

BALANCE
FINISH
BODY
PEATY / SMOKY
SHARP / ACIDIC
ASTRINGENT
ROASTED / WOODY
MOLASSES
SWEET / CANDIED
SPICES
HERBAL / VEGETAL
DRIED FRUIT
CITRUS FRUIT
DARK FRUIT
FRESH FRUIT

FLAVOR NOTES

SMELL / SCENT NOTES

OTHER NOTES

RUM NAME		DATE TASTED

PRODUCER	DISTILLERY

TYPE / GRADE	COUNTRY OF ORIGIN

STILL TYPE	REGION

AGE	ALCOHOL %	PRICE	BOTTLE SIZE

QUALITY RATING

1	2	3	4	5	6	7	8	9	10

VALUE FOR MONEY

1	2	3	4	5	6	7	8	9	10

COLOR METER

BLACK
DARK BROWN
MAHOGANY
BRICK
DARK AMBER
AMBER
GOLD
STRAW
CLEAR

FLAVOR WHEEL

BALANCE · HEAT / ABM ____ % · FINISH · FRESH FRUIT · BODY · DARK FRUIT · PEATY / SMOKY · CITRUS FRUIT · SHARP / ACIDIC · DRIED FRUIT · ASTRINGENT · HERBAL / VEGETAL · ROASTED / WOODY · SPICES · MOLASSES · SWEET / CANDIED

FLAVOR NOTES

SMELL / SCENT NOTES

OTHER NOTES

RUM LOG

RUM NAME		DATE TASTED

PRODUCER	DISTILLERY

TYPE / GRADE	COUNTRY OF ORIGIN

STILL TYPE	REGION

AGE	ALCOHOL %	PRICE	BOTTLE SIZE

QUALITY RATING

1	2	3	4	5	6	7	8	9	10

VALUE FOR MONEY

1	2	3	4	5	6	7	8	9	10

COLOR METER

- BLACK
- DARK BROWN
- MAHOGANY
- BRICK
- DARK AMBER
- AMBER
- GOLD
- STRAW
- CLEAR

FLAVOR WHEEL

HEAT / ABM _____ %

BALANCE
FINISH
BODY
PEATY / SMOKY
SHARP / ACIDIC
ASTRINGENT
ROASTED / WOODY
MOLASSES
SWEET / CANDIED
SPICES
HERBAL / VEGETAL
DRIED FRUIT
CITRUS FRUIT
DARK FRUIT
FRESH FRUIT

FLAVOR NOTES

SMELL / SCENT NOTES

OTHER NOTES

32

RUM NAME	DATE TASTED

PRODUCER	DISTILLERY

TYPE / GRADE	COUNTRY OF ORIGIN

STILL TYPE	REGION

AGE	ALCOHOL %	PRICE	BOTTLE SIZE

QUALITY RATING

1	2	3	4	5	6	7	8	9	10

VALUE FOR MONEY

1	2	3	4	5	6	7	8	9	10

COLOR METER

- BLACK
- DARK BROWN
- MAHOGANY
- BRICK
- DARK AMBER
- AMBER
- GOLD
- STRAW
- CLEAR

FLAVOR WHEEL

HEAT / ABM _____ %

BALANCE
FINISH
BODY
PEATY / SMOKY
SHARP / ACIDIC
ASTRINGENT
ROASTED / WOODY
MOLASSES
SWEET / CANDIED
SPICES
HERBAL / VEGETAL
DRIED FRUIT
CITRUS FRUIT
DARK FRUIT
FRESH FRUIT

FLAVOR NOTES

SMELL / SCENT NOTES

OTHER NOTES

RUM LOG

RUM NAME		DATE TASTED

PRODUCER	DISTILLERY

TYPE / GRADE	COUNTRY OF ORIGIN

STILL TYPE	REGION

AGE	ALCOHOL %	PRICE	BOTTLE SIZE

QUALITY RATING

1	2	3	4	5	6	7	8	9	10

VALUE FOR MONEY

1	2	3	4	5	6	7	8	9	10

COLOR METER

- BLACK
- DARK BROWN
- MAHOGANY
- BRICK
- DARK AMBER
- AMBER
- GOLD
- STRAW
- CLEAR

FLAVOR WHEEL

BALANCE
HEAT / ABM _____ %
FINISH
FRESH FRUIT
BODY
PEATY / SMOKY
DARK FRUIT
SHARP / ACIDIC
CITRUS FRUIT
ASTRINGENT
DRIED FRUIT
ROASTED / WOODY
HERBAL / VEGETAL
MOLASSES
SPICES
SWEET / CANDIED

FLAVOR NOTES

SMELL / SCENT NOTES

OTHER NOTES

RUM NAME		DATE TASTED

PRODUCER	DISTILLERY

TYPE / GRADE	COUNTRY OF ORIGIN

STILL TYPE	REGION

AGE	ALCOHOL %	PRICE	BOTTLE SIZE

QUALITY RATING

1	2	3	4	5	6	7	8	9	10

VALUE FOR MONEY

1	2	3	4	5	6	7	8	9	10

COLOR METER

- BLACK
- DARK BROWN
- MAHOGANY
- BRICK
- DARK AMBER
- AMBER
- GOLD
- STRAW
- CLEAR

FLAVOR WHEEL

BALANCE — HEAT / ABM _____ %

FINISH, BODY, PEATY / SMOKY, SHARP / ACIDIC, ASTRINGENT, ROASTED / WOODY, MOLASSES, SWEET / CANDIED, SPICES, HERBAL / VEGETAL, DRIED FRUIT, CITRUS FRUIT, DARK FRUIT, FRESH FRUIT

FLAVOR NOTES

SMELL / SCENT NOTES

OTHER NOTES

RUM LOG

RUM NAME		DATE TASTED

PRODUCER	DISTILLERY

TYPE / GRADE	COUNTRY OF ORIGIN

STILL TYPE	REGION

AGE	ALCOHOL %	PRICE	BOTTLE SIZE

QUALITY RATING	VALUE FOR MONEY

1	2	3	4	5	6	7	8	9	10

1	2	3	4	5	6	7	8	9	10

COLOR METER

- BLACK
- DARK BROWN
- MAHOGANY
- BRICK
- DARK AMBER
- AMBER
- GOLD
- STRAW
- CLEAR

FLAVOR WHEEL

HEAT / ABM _____ %

BALANCE
FINISH
BODY
PEATY / SMOKY
SHARP / ACIDIC
ASTRINGENT
ROASTED / WOODY
MOLASSES
SWEET / CANDIED
SPICES
HERBAL / VEGETAL
DRIED FRUIT
CITRUS FRUIT
DARK FRUIT
FRESH FRUIT

FLAVOR NOTES

SMELL / SCENT NOTES

OTHER NOTES

RUM NAME		DATE TASTED
PRODUCER	DISTILLERY	
TYPE / GRADE	COUNTRY OF ORIGIN	
STILL TYPE	REGION	

AGE	ALCOHOL %	PRICE	BOTTLE SIZE

QUALITY RATING

1	2	3	4	5	6	7	8	9	10

VALUE FOR MONEY

1	2	3	4	5	6	7	8	9	10

COLOR METER

- BLACK
- DARK BROWN
- MAHOGANY
- BRICK
- DARK AMBER
- AMBER
- GOLD
- STRAW
- CLEAR

FLAVOR WHEEL

HEAT / ABM _____ %

BALANCE
FINISH
BODY
PEATY / SMOKY
SHARP / ACIDIC
ASTRINGENT
ROASTED / WOODY
MOLASSES
SWEET / CANDIED
SPICES
HERBAL / VEGETAL
DRIED FRUIT
CITRUS FRUIT
DARK FRUIT
FRESH FRUIT

FLAVOR NOTES

SMELL / SCENT NOTES

OTHER NOTES

RUM LOG

RUM NAME		DATE TASTED
PRODUCER		DISTILLERY
TYPE / GRADE		COUNTRY OF ORIGIN
STILL TYPE		REGION

AGE	ALCOHOL %	PRICE	BOTTLE SIZE

QUALITY RATING

1	2	3	4	5	6	7	8	9	10

VALUE FOR MONEY

1	2	3	4	5	6	7	8	9	10

COLOR METER

- BLACK
- DARK BROWN
- MAHOGANY
- BRICK
- DARK AMBER
- AMBER
- GOLD
- STRAW
- CLEAR

FLAVOR WHEEL

BALANCE HEAT / ABM _____ %
FINISH
BODY
FRESH FRUIT
PEATY / SMOKY
DARK FRUIT
SHARP / ACIDIC
CITRUS FRUIT
ASTRINGENT
DRIED FRUIT
ROASTED / WOODY
HERBAL / VEGETAL
MOLASSES
SPICES
SWEET / CANDIED

FLAVOR NOTES

SMELL / SCENT NOTES

OTHER NOTES

RUM NAME	DATE TASTED

PRODUCER	DISTILLERY

TYPE / GRADE	COUNTRY OF ORIGIN

STILL TYPE	REGION

AGE	ALCOHOL %	PRICE	BOTTLE SIZE

QUALITY RATING

1	2	3	4	5	6	7	8	9	10

VALUE FOR MONEY

1	2	3	4	5	6	7	8	9	10

COLOR METER

- BLACK
- DARK BROWN
- MAHOGANY
- BRICK
- DARK AMBER
- AMBER
- GOLD
- STRAW
- CLEAR

FLAVOR WHEEL

HEAT / ABM _____ %

BALANCE, FINISH, BODY, PEATY / SMOKY, SHARP / ACIDIC, ASTRINGENT, ROASTED / WOODY, MOLASSES, SWEET / CANDIED, SPICES, HERBAL / VEGETAL, DRIED FRUIT, CITRUS FRUIT, DARK FRUIT, FRESH FRUIT

FLAVOR NOTES

SMELL / SCENT NOTES	OTHER NOTES

RUM LOG

RUM NAME	DATE TASTED

PRODUCER	DISTILLERY

TYPE / GRADE	COUNTRY OF ORIGIN

STILL TYPE	REGION

AGE	ALCOHOL %	PRICE	BOTTLE SIZE

QUALITY RATING

1	2	3	4	5	6	7	8	9	10

VALUE FOR MONEY

1	2	3	4	5	6	7	8	9	10

COLOR METER

- BLACK
- DARK BROWN
- MAHOGANY
- BRICK
- DARK AMBER
- AMBER
- GOLD
- STRAW
- CLEAR

FLAVOR WHEEL

BALANCE / HEAT / ABM _____ %
FINISH
BODY
PEATY / SMOKY
SHARP / ACIDIC
ASTRINGENT
ROASTED / WOODY
MOLASSES
SWEET / CANDIED
SPICES
HERBAL / VEGETAL
DRIED FRUIT
CITRUS FRUIT
DARK FRUIT
FRESH FRUIT

FLAVOR NOTES

SMELL / SCENT NOTES

OTHER NOTES

RUM NAME	DATE TASTED

PRODUCER	DISTILLERY

TYPE / GRADE	COUNTRY OF ORIGIN

STILL TYPE	REGION

AGE	ALCOHOL %	PRICE	BOTTLE SIZE

QUALITY RATING

1	2	3	4	5	6	7	8	9	10

VALUE FOR MONEY

1	2	3	4	5	6	7	8	9	10

COLOR METER

- BLACK
- DARK BROWN
- MAHOGANY
- BRICK
- DARK AMBER
- AMBER
- GOLD
- STRAW
- CLEAR

FLAVOR WHEEL

HEAT / ABM _____ %

BALANCE, FINISH, BODY, PEATY / SMOKY, SHARP / ACIDIC, ASTRINGENT, ROASTED / WOODY, MOLASSES, SWEET / CANDIED, SPICES, HERBAL / VEGETAL, DRIED FRUIT, CITRUS FRUIT, DARK FRUIT, FRESH FRUIT

FLAVOR NOTES

SMELL / SCENT NOTES

OTHER NOTES

RUM LOG

RUM NAME		DATE TASTED

PRODUCER	DISTILLERY

TYPE / GRADE	COUNTRY OF ORIGIN

STILL TYPE	REGION

AGE	ALCOHOL %	PRICE	BOTTLE SIZE

QUALITY RATING	VALUE FOR MONEY

1	2	3	4	5	6	7	8	9	10

1	2	3	4	5	6	7	8	9	10

COLOR METER

- BLACK
- DARK BROWN
- MAHOGANY
- BRICK
- DARK AMBER
- AMBER
- GOLD
- STRAW
- CLEAR

FLAVOR WHEEL

BALANCE HEAT / ABM _____ %
FINISH
BODY
PEATY / SMOKY
SHARP / ACIDIC
ASTRINGENT
ROASTED / WOODY
MOLASSES
SWEET / CANDIED
SPICES
HERBAL / VEGETAL
DRIED FRUIT
CITRUS FRUIT
DARK FRUIT
FRESH FRUIT

FLAVOR NOTES

SMELL / SCENT NOTES

OTHER NOTES

RUM NAME

DATE TASTED

PRODUCER

DISTILLERY

TYPE / GRADE

COUNTRY OF ORIGIN

STILL TYPE

REGION

AGE	ALCOHOL %	PRICE	BOTTLE SIZE

QUALITY RATING

1	2	3	4	5	6	7	8	9	10

VALUE FOR MONEY

1	2	3	4	5	6	7	8	9	10

COLOR METER

BLACK
DARK BROWN
MAHOGANY
BRICK
DARK AMBER
AMBER
GOLD
STRAW
CLEAR

FLAVOR WHEEL

BALANCE, HEAT / ABM ____ %, FINISH, FRESH FRUIT, BODY, DARK FRUIT, PEATY / SMOKY, CITRUS FRUIT, SHARP / ACIDIC, DRIED FRUIT, ASTRINGENT, HERBAL / VEGETAL, ROASTED / WOODY, SPICES, MOLASSES, SWEET / CANDIED

FLAVOR NOTES

SMELL / SCENT NOTES

OTHER NOTES

RUM LOG

RUM NAME	DATE TASTED

PRODUCER	DISTILLERY

TYPE / GRADE	COUNTRY OF ORIGIN

STILL TYPE	REGION

AGE	ALCOHOL %	PRICE	BOTTLE SIZE

QUALITY RATING

1	2	3	4	5	6	7	8	9	10

VALUE FOR MONEY

1	2	3	4	5	6	7	8	9	10

COLOR METER

- BLACK
- DARK BROWN
- MAHOGANY
- BRICK
- DARK AMBER
- AMBER
- GOLD
- STRAW
- CLEAR

FLAVOR WHEEL

HEAT / ABM _____ %

BALANCE
FINISH
BODY
FRESH FRUIT
PEATY / SMOKY
DARK FRUIT
SHARP / ACIDIC
CITRUS FRUIT
ASTRINGENT
DRIED FRUIT
ROASTED / WOODY
HERBAL / VEGETAL
MOLASSES
SPICES
SWEET / CANDIED

FLAVOR NOTES

SMELL / SCENT NOTES

OTHER NOTES

RUM NAME		DATE TASTED

PRODUCER	DISTILLERY

TYPE / GRADE	COUNTRY OF ORIGIN

STILL TYPE	REGION

AGE	ALCOHOL %	PRICE	BOTTLE SIZE

QUALITY RATING

1	2	3	4	5	6	7	8	9	10

VALUE FOR MONEY

1	2	3	4	5	6	7	8	9	10

COLOR METER

BLACK
DARK BROWN
MAHOGANY
BRICK
DARK AMBER
AMBER
GOLD
STRAW
CLEAR

FLAVOR WHEEL

HEAT / ABM _____ %
BALANCE
FINISH
FRESH FRUIT
BODY
DARK FRUIT
PEATY / SMOKY
CITRUS FRUIT
SHARP / ACIDIC
DRIED FRUIT
ASTRINGENT
ROASTED / WOODY
HERBAL / VEGETAL
MOLASSES
SPICES
SWEET / CANDIED

FLAVOR NOTES

SMELL / SCENT NOTES

OTHER NOTES

RUM LOG

RUM NAME	DATE TASTED

PRODUCER	DISTILLERY

TYPE / GRADE	COUNTRY OF ORIGIN

STILL TYPE	REGION

AGE	ALCOHOL %	PRICE	BOTTLE SIZE

QUALITY RATING

1	2	3	4	5	6	7	8	9	10

VALUE FOR MONEY

1	2	3	4	5	6	7	8	9	10

COLOR METER

- BLACK
- DARK BROWN
- MAHOGANY
- BRICK
- DARK AMBER
- AMBER
- GOLD
- STRAW
- CLEAR

FLAVOR WHEEL

HEAT / ABM _____ %

BALANCE, FINISH, BODY, PEATY / SMOKY, SHARP / ACIDIC, ASTRINGENT, ROASTED / WOODY, MOLASSES, SWEET / CANDIED, SPICES, HERBAL / VEGETAL, DRIED FRUIT, CITRUS FRUIT, DARK FRUIT, FRESH FRUIT

FLAVOR NOTES

SMELL / SCENT NOTES

OTHER NOTES

RUM NAME	DATE TASTED

PRODUCER	DISTILLERY

TYPE / GRADE	COUNTRY OF ORIGIN

STILL TYPE	REGION

AGE	ALCOHOL %	PRICE	BOTTLE SIZE

QUALITY RATING

1	2	3	4	5	6	7	8	9	10

VALUE FOR MONEY

1	2	3	4	5	6	7	8	9	10

COLOR METER

- BLACK
- DARK BROWN
- MAHOGANY
- BRICK
- DARK AMBER
- AMBER
- GOLD
- STRAW
- CLEAR

FLAVOR WHEEL

HEAT / ABM _____ %

BALANCE, FINISH, BODY, PEATY / SMOKY, SHARP / ACIDIC, ASTRINGENT, ROASTED / WOODY, MOLASSES, SWEET / CANDIED, SPICES, HERBAL / VEGETAL, DRIED FRUIT, CITRUS FRUIT, DARK FRUIT, FRESH FRUIT

FLAVOR NOTES

SMELL / SCENT NOTES

OTHER NOTES

RUM LOG

RUM NAME	DATE TASTED

PRODUCER	DISTILLERY

TYPE / GRADE	COUNTRY OF ORIGIN

STILL TYPE	REGION

AGE	ALCOHOL %	PRICE	BOTTLE SIZE

QUALITY RATING

1	2	3	4	5	6	7	8	9	10

VALUE FOR MONEY

1	2	3	4	5	6	7	8	9	10

COLOR METER

- BLACK
- DARK BROWN
- MAHOGANY
- BRICK
- DARK AMBER
- AMBER
- GOLD
- STRAW
- CLEAR

FLAVOR WHEEL

HEAT / ABM _____ %

BALANCE, FINISH, BODY, PEATY / SMOKY, SHARP / ACIDIC, ASTRINGENT, ROASTED / WOODY, MOLASSES, SWEET / CANDIED, SPICES, HERBAL / VEGETAL, DRIED FRUIT, CITRUS FRUIT, DARK FRUIT, FRESH FRUIT

FLAVOR NOTES

SMELL / SCENT NOTES	OTHER NOTES

RUM NAME		DATE TASTED
PRODUCER	**DISTILLERY**	
TYPE / GRADE	**COUNTRY OF ORIGIN**	
STILL TYPE	**REGION**	

AGE	ALCOHOL %	PRICE	BOTTLE SIZE

QUALITY RATING

1	2	3	4	5	6	7	8	9	10

VALUE FOR MONEY

1	2	3	4	5	6	7	8	9	10

COLOR METER

BLACK

DARK BROWN

MAHOGANY

BRICK

DARK AMBER

AMBER

GOLD

STRAW

CLEAR

FLAVOR WHEEL

HEAT / %
ABM _____

BALANCE

FINISH

BODY

FRESH FRUIT

PEATY / SMOKY

DARK FRUIT

SHARP / ACIDIC

CITRUS FRUIT

ASTRINGENT

DRIED FRUIT

ROASTED / WOODY

HERBAL / VEGETAL

MOLASSES

SPICES

SWEET / CANDIED

FLAVOR NOTES

SMELL / SCENT NOTES

OTHER NOTES

RUM LOG

RUM NAME	DATE TASTED

PRODUCER	DISTILLERY

TYPE / GRADE	COUNTRY OF ORIGIN

STILL TYPE	REGION

AGE	ALCOHOL %	PRICE	BOTTLE SIZE

QUALITY RATING

1	2	3	4	5	6	7	8	9	10

VALUE FOR MONEY

1	2	3	4	5	6	7	8	9	10

COLOR METER

- BLACK
- DARK BROWN
- MAHOGANY
- BRICK
- DARK AMBER
- AMBER
- GOLD
- STRAW
- CLEAR

FLAVOR WHEEL

HEAT / ABM _____ %

BALANCE, FINISH, BODY, PEATY / SMOKY, SHARP / ACIDIC, ASTRINGENT, ROASTED / WOODY, MOLASSES, SWEET / CANDIED, SPICES, HERBAL / VEGETAL, DRIED FRUIT, CITRUS FRUIT, DARK FRUIT, FRESH FRUIT

FLAVOR NOTES

SMELL / SCENT NOTES

OTHER NOTES

RUM NAME		DATE TASTED

PRODUCER	DISTILLERY

TYPE / GRADE	COUNTRY OF ORIGIN

STILL TYPE	REGION

AGE	ALCOHOL %	PRICE	BOTTLE SIZE

QUALITY RATING

1	2	3	4	5	6	7	8	9	10

VALUE FOR MONEY

1	2	3	4	5	6	7	8	9	10

COLOR METER

BLACK
DARK BROWN
MAHOGANY
BRICK
DARK AMBER
AMBER
GOLD
STRAW
CLEAR

FLAVOR WHEEL

BALANCE, HEAT / ABM ____ %, FINISH, FRESH FRUIT, BODY, DARK FRUIT, PEATY / SMOKY, CITRUS FRUIT, SHARP / ACIDIC, DRIED FRUIT, ASTRINGENT, HERBAL / VEGETAL, ROASTED / WOODY, SPICES, MOLASSES, SWEET / CANDIED

FLAVOR NOTES

SMELL / SCENT NOTES

OTHER NOTES

RUM LOG

RUM NAME	DATE TASTED

PRODUCER	DISTILLERY

TYPE / GRADE	COUNTRY OF ORIGIN

STILL TYPE	REGION

AGE	ALCOHOL %	PRICE	BOTTLE SIZE

QUALITY RATING

1	2	3	4	5	6	7	8	9	10

VALUE FOR MONEY

1	2	3	4	5	6	7	8	9	10

COLOR METER

- BLACK
- DARK BROWN
- MAHOGANY
- BRICK
- DARK AMBER
- AMBER
- GOLD
- STRAW
- CLEAR

FLAVOR WHEEL

BALANCE, HEAT / ABM _____ %, FINISH, FRESH FRUIT, BODY, DARK FRUIT, PEATY / SMOKY, CITRUS FRUIT, SHARP / ACIDIC, DRIED FRUIT, ASTRINGENT, HERBAL / VEGETAL, ROASTED / WOODY, SPICES, MOLASSES, SWEET / CANDIED

FLAVOR NOTES

SMELL / SCENT NOTES

OTHER NOTES

RUM NAME		DATE TASTED

PRODUCER	DISTILLERY

TYPE / GRADE	COUNTRY OF ORIGIN

STILL TYPE	REGION

AGE	ALCOHOL %	PRICE	BOTTLE SIZE

QUALITY RATING

1	2	3	4	5	6	7	8	9	10

VALUE FOR MONEY

1	2	3	4	5	6	7	8	9	10

COLOR METER

BLACK
DARK BROWN
MAHOGANY
BRICK
DARK AMBER
AMBER
GOLD
STRAW
CLEAR

FLAVOR WHEEL

BALANCE, HEAT / ABM _____ %, FINISH, BODY, FRESH FRUIT, PEATY / SMOKY, DARK FRUIT, SHARP / ACIDIC, CITRUS FRUIT, ASTRINGENT, DRIED FRUIT, ROASTED / WOODY, HERBAL / VEGETAL, MOLASSES, SPICES, SWEET / CANDIED

FLAVOR NOTES

SMELL / SCENT NOTES

OTHER NOTES

RUM LOG

RUM NAME		DATE TASTED

PRODUCER	DISTILLERY

TYPE / GRADE	COUNTRY OF ORIGIN

STILL TYPE	REGION

AGE	ALCOHOL %	PRICE	BOTTLE SIZE

QUALITY RATING

1	2	3	4	5	6	7	8	9	10

VALUE FOR MONEY

1	2	3	4	5	6	7	8	9	10

COLOR METER

- BLACK
- DARK BROWN
- MAHOGANY
- BRICK
- DARK AMBER
- AMBER
- GOLD
- STRAW
- CLEAR

FLAVOR WHEEL

HEAT / ABM _____ %

BALANCE, FINISH, BODY, PEATY / SMOKY, SHARP / ACIDIC, ASTRINGENT, ROASTED / WOODY, MOLASSES, SWEET / CANDIED, SPICES, HERBAL / VEGETAL, DRIED FRUIT, CITRUS FRUIT, DARK FRUIT, FRESH FRUIT

FLAVOR NOTES

SMELL / SCENT NOTES

OTHER NOTES

RUM NAME	DATE TASTED

PRODUCER	DISTILLERY

TYPE / GRADE	COUNTRY OF ORIGIN

STILL TYPE	REGION

AGE	ALCOHOL %	PRICE	BOTTLE SIZE

QUALITY RATING

1	2	3	4	5	6	7	8	9	10

VALUE FOR MONEY

1	2	3	4	5	6	7	8	9	10

COLOR METER

- BLACK
- DARK BROWN
- MAHOGANY
- BRICK
- DARK AMBER
- AMBER
- GOLD
- STRAW
- CLEAR

FLAVOR WHEEL

HEAT / ABM _____ %

BALANCE
FINISH
BODY
PEATY / SMOKY
SHARP / ACIDIC
ASTRINGENT
ROASTED / WOODY
MOLASSES
SWEET / CANDIED
SPICES
HERBAL / VEGETAL
DRIED FRUIT
CITRUS FRUIT
DARK FRUIT
FRESH FRUIT

FLAVOR NOTES

SMELL / SCENT NOTES	OTHER NOTES

RUM LOG

RUM NAME	DATE TASTED

PRODUCER	DISTILLERY

TYPE / GRADE	COUNTRY OF ORIGIN

STILL TYPE	REGION

AGE	ALCOHOL %	PRICE	BOTTLE SIZE

QUALITY RATING

1	2	3	4	5	6	7	8	9	10

VALUE FOR MONEY

1	2	3	4	5	6	7	8	9	10

COLOR METER

- BLACK
- DARK BROWN
- MAHOGANY
- BRICK
- DARK AMBER
- AMBER
- GOLD
- STRAW
- CLEAR

FLAVOR WHEEL

HEAT / ABM _____ %

BALANCE
FINISH
BODY
PEATY / SMOKY
SHARP / ACIDIC
ASTRINGENT
ROASTED / WOODY
MOLASSES
SWEET / CANDIED
SPICES
HERBAL / VEGETAL
DRIED FRUIT
CITRUS FRUIT
DARK FRUIT
FRESH FRUIT

FLAVOR NOTES

SMELL / SCENT NOTES

OTHER NOTES

RUM NAME	DATE TASTED

PRODUCER	DISTILLERY

TYPE / GRADE	COUNTRY OF ORIGIN

STILL TYPE	REGION

AGE	ALCOHOL %	PRICE	BOTTLE SIZE

QUALITY RATING

1	2	3	4	5	6	7	8	9	10

VALUE FOR MONEY

1	2	3	4	5	6	7	8	9	10

COLOR METER

- BLACK
- DARK BROWN
- MAHOGANY
- BRICK
- DARK AMBER
- AMBER
- GOLD
- STRAW
- CLEAR

FLAVOR WHEEL

HEAT / ABM _____ %

BALANCE
FINISH
BODY
PEATY / SMOKY
SHARP / ACIDIC
ASTRINGENT
ROASTED / WOODY
MOLASSES
SWEET / CANDIED
SPICES
HERBAL / VEGETAL
DRIED FRUIT
CITRUS FRUIT
DARK FRUIT
FRESH FRUIT

FLAVOR NOTES

SMELL / SCENT NOTES

OTHER NOTES

RUM LOG

RUM NAME	DATE TASTED

PRODUCER	DISTILLERY

TYPE / GRADE	COUNTRY OF ORIGIN

STILL TYPE	REGION

AGE	ALCOHOL %	PRICE	BOTTLE SIZE

QUALITY RATING

1	2	3	4	5	6	7	8	9	10

VALUE FOR MONEY

1	2	3	4	5	6	7	8	9	10

COLOR METER

- BLACK
- DARK BROWN
- MAHOGANY
- BRICK
- DARK AMBER
- AMBER
- GOLD
- STRAW
- CLEAR

FLAVOR WHEEL

HEAT / ABM _____ %

BALANCE
FINISH
BODY
PEATY / SMOKY
SHARP / ACIDIC
ASTRINGENT
ROASTED / WOODY
MOLASSES
SWEET / CANDIED
SPICES
HERBAL / VEGETAL
DRIED FRUIT
CITRUS FRUIT
DARK FRUIT
FRESH FRUIT

FLAVOR NOTES

SMELL / SCENT NOTES

OTHER NOTES

RUM NAME		DATE TASTED

PRODUCER	DISTILLERY

TYPE / GRADE	COUNTRY OF ORIGIN

STILL TYPE	REGION

AGE	ALCOHOL %	PRICE	BOTTLE SIZE

QUALITY RATING

1	2	3	4	5	6	7	8	9	10

VALUE FOR MONEY

1	2	3	4	5	6	7	8	9	10

COLOR METER

- BLACK
- DARK BROWN
- MAHOGANY
- BRICK
- DARK AMBER
- AMBER
- GOLD
- STRAW
- CLEAR

FLAVOR WHEEL

HEAT / ABM _____ %

BALANCE, FINISH, BODY, PEATY / SMOKY, SHARP / ACIDIC, ASTRINGENT, ROASTED / WOODY, MOLASSES, SWEET / CANDIED, SPICES, HERBAL / VEGETAL, DRIED FRUIT, CITRUS FRUIT, DARK FRUIT, FRESH FRUIT

FLAVOR NOTES

SMELL / SCENT NOTES

OTHER NOTES

RUM LOG

RUM NAME		DATE TASTED

PRODUCER	DISTILLERY

TYPE / GRADE	COUNTRY OF ORIGIN

STILL TYPE	REGION

AGE	ALCOHOL %	PRICE	BOTTLE SIZE

QUALITY RATING

1	2	3	4	5	6	7	8	9	10

VALUE FOR MONEY

1	2	3	4	5	6	7	8	9	10

COLOR METER

- BLACK
- DARK BROWN
- MAHOGANY
- BRICK
- DARK AMBER
- AMBER
- GOLD
- STRAW
- CLEAR

FLAVOR WHEEL

HEAT / ABM _____ %

BALANCE
FINISH
BODY
PEATY / SMOKY
SHARP / ACIDIC
ASTRINGENT
ROASTED / WOODY
MOLASSES
SWEET / CANDIED
SPICES
HERBAL / VEGETAL
DRIED FRUIT
CITRUS FRUIT
DARK FRUIT
FRESH FRUIT

FLAVOR NOTES

SMELL / SCENT NOTES

OTHER NOTES

RUM NAME		DATE TASTED

PRODUCER	DISTILLERY

TYPE / GRADE	COUNTRY OF ORIGIN

STILL TYPE	REGION

AGE	ALCOHOL %	PRICE	BOTTLE SIZE

QUALITY RATING

1	2	3	4	5	6	7	8	9	10

VALUE FOR MONEY

1	2	3	4	5	6	7	8	9	10

COLOR METER

- BLACK
- DARK BROWN
- MAHOGANY
- BRICK
- DARK AMBER
- AMBER
- GOLD
- STRAW
- CLEAR

FLAVOR WHEEL

BALANCE, HEAT / ABM ____ %, FINISH, FRESH FRUIT, BODY, DARK FRUIT, PEATY / SMOKY, CITRUS FRUIT, SHARP / ACIDIC, DRIED FRUIT, ASTRINGENT, HERBAL / VEGETAL, ROASTED / WOODY, SPICES, MOLASSES, SWEET / CANDIED

FLAVOR NOTES

SMELL / SCENT NOTES

OTHER NOTES

RUM LOG

RUM NAME	DATE TASTED

PRODUCER	DISTILLERY

TYPE / GRADE	COUNTRY OF ORIGIN

STILL TYPE	REGION

AGE	ALCOHOL %	PRICE	BOTTLE SIZE

QUALITY RATING

1	2	3	4	5	6	7	8	9	10

VALUE FOR MONEY

1	2	3	4	5	6	7	8	9	10

COLOR METER

- BLACK
- DARK BROWN
- MAHOGANY
- BRICK
- DARK AMBER
- AMBER
- GOLD
- STRAW
- CLEAR

FLAVOR WHEEL

HEAT / ABM _____ %

BALANCE
FINISH
BODY
PEATY / SMOKY
SHARP / ACIDIC
ASTRINGENT
ROASTED / WOODY
MOLASSES
SWEET / CANDIED
SPICES
HERBAL / VEGETAL
DRIED FRUIT
CITRUS FRUIT
DARK FRUIT
FRESH FRUIT

FLAVOR NOTES

SMELL / SCENT NOTES

OTHER NOTES

RUM NAME

DATE TASTED

PRODUCER

DISTILLERY

TYPE / GRADE

COUNTRY OF ORIGIN

STILL TYPE

REGION

AGE	ALCOHOL %	PRICE	BOTTLE SIZE

QUALITY RATING

1	2	3	4	5	6	7	8	9	10

VALUE FOR MONEY

1	2	3	4	5	6	7	8	9	10

COLOR METER

BLACK
DARK BROWN
MAHOGANY
BRICK
DARK AMBER
AMBER
GOLD
STRAW
CLEAR

FLAVOR WHEEL

HEAT / ABM _____ %
BALANCE
FINISH
BODY
FRESH FRUIT
PEATY / SMOKY
DARK FRUIT
SHARP / ACIDIC
CITRUS FRUIT
ASTRINGENT
DRIED FRUIT
ROASTED / WOODY
HERBAL / VEGETAL
MOLASSES
SPICES
SWEET / CANDIED

FLAVOR NOTES

SMELL / SCENT NOTES

OTHER NOTES

RUM LOG

RUM NAME	DATE TASTED

PRODUCER	DISTILLERY

TYPE / GRADE	COUNTRY OF ORIGIN

STILL TYPE	REGION

AGE	ALCOHOL %	PRICE	BOTTLE SIZE

QUALITY RATING

1	2	3	4	5	6	7	8	9	10

VALUE FOR MONEY

1	2	3	4	5	6	7	8	9	10

COLOR METER

- BLACK
- DARK BROWN
- MAHOGANY
- BRICK
- DARK AMBER
- AMBER
- GOLD
- STRAW
- CLEAR

FLAVOR WHEEL

HEAT / ABM _____ %

BALANCE
FINISH
BODY
PEATY / SMOKY
SHARP / ACIDIC
ASTRINGENT
ROASTED / WOODY
MOLASSES
SWEET / CANDIED
SPICES
HERBAL / VEGETAL
DRIED FRUIT
CITRUS FRUIT
DARK FRUIT
FRESH FRUIT

FLAVOR NOTES

SMELL / SCENT NOTES

OTHER NOTES

RUM NAME		DATE TASTED

PRODUCER	DISTILLERY

TYPE / GRADE	COUNTRY OF ORIGIN

STILL TYPE	REGION

AGE	ALCOHOL %	PRICE	BOTTLE SIZE

QUALITY RATING

1	2	3	4	5	6	7	8	9	10

VALUE FOR MONEY

1	2	3	4	5	6	7	8	9	10

COLOR METER

BLACK

DARK BROWN

MAHOGANY

BRICK

DARK AMBER

AMBER

GOLD

STRAW

CLEAR

FLAVOR WHEEL

HEAT / ABM _____ %

BALANCE

FINISH

BODY

PEATY / SMOKY

SHARP / ACIDIC

ASTRINGENT

ROASTED / WOODY

MOLASSES

SWEET / CANDIED

SPICES

HERBAL / VEGETAL

DRIED FRUIT

CITRUS FRUIT

DARK FRUIT

FRESH FRUIT

FLAVOR NOTES

SMELL / SCENT NOTES

OTHER NOTES

RUM LOG

RUM NAME		DATE TASTED

PRODUCER	DISTILLERY

TYPE / GRADE	COUNTRY OF ORIGIN

STILL TYPE	REGION

AGE	ALCOHOL %	PRICE	BOTTLE SIZE

QUALITY RATING

1	2	3	4	5	6	7	8	9	10

VALUE FOR MONEY

1	2	3	4	5	6	7	8	9	10

COLOR METER

BLACK

DARK BROWN

MAHOGANY

BRICK

DARK AMBER

AMBER

GOLD

STRAW

CLEAR

FLAVOR WHEEL

HEAT / ABM _____ %

BALANCE
FINISH
BODY
PEATY / SMOKY
SHARP / ACIDIC
ASTRINGENT
ROASTED / WOODY
MOLASSES
SWEET / CANDIED
SPICES
HERBAL / VEGETAL
DRIED FRUIT
CITRUS FRUIT
DARK FRUIT
FRESH FRUIT

FLAVOR NOTES

SMELL / SCENT NOTES

OTHER NOTES

RUM NAME		DATE TASTED

PRODUCER	DISTILLERY

TYPE / GRADE	COUNTRY OF ORIGIN

STILL TYPE	REGION

AGE	ALCOHOL %	PRICE	BOTTLE SIZE

QUALITY RATING

1	2	3	4	5	6	7	8	9	10

VALUE FOR MONEY

1	2	3	4	5	6	7	8	9	10

COLOR METER

BLACK
DARK BROWN
MAHOGANY
BRICK
DARK AMBER
AMBER
GOLD
STRAW
CLEAR

FLAVOR WHEEL

BALANCE, HEAT / ABM ____ %, FINISH, FRESH FRUIT, BODY, DARK FRUIT, PEATY / SMOKY, CITRUS FRUIT, SHARP / ACIDIC, DRIED FRUIT, ASTRINGENT, HERBAL / VEGETAL, ROASTED / WOODY, SPICES, MOLASSES, SWEET / CANDIED

FLAVOR NOTES

SMELL / SCENT NOTES

OTHER NOTES

RUM LOG

RUM NAME		DATE TASTED

PRODUCER	DISTILLERY

TYPE / GRADE	COUNTRY OF ORIGIN

STILL TYPE	REGION

AGE	ALCOHOL %	PRICE	BOTTLE SIZE

QUALITY RATING

1	2	3	4	5	6	7	8	9	10

VALUE FOR MONEY

1	2	3	4	5	6	7	8	9	10

COLOR METER

- BLACK
- DARK BROWN
- MAHOGANY
- BRICK
- DARK AMBER
- AMBER
- GOLD
- STRAW
- CLEAR

FLAVOR WHEEL

HEAT / ABM _____ %

BALANCE
FINISH
BODY
PEATY / SMOKY
SHARP / ACIDIC
ASTRINGENT
ROASTED / WOODY
MOLASSES
SWEET / CANDIED
SPICES
HERBAL / VEGETAL
DRIED FRUIT
CITRUS FRUIT
DARK FRUIT
FRESH FRUIT

FLAVOR NOTES

SMELL / SCENT NOTES

OTHER NOTES

RUM NAME		DATE TASTED

PRODUCER	DISTILLERY

TYPE / GRADE	COUNTRY OF ORIGIN

STILL TYPE	REGION

AGE	ALCOHOL %	PRICE	BOTTLE SIZE

QUALITY RATING

1	2	3	4	5	6	7	8	9	10

VALUE FOR MONEY

1	2	3	4	5	6	7	8	9	10

COLOR METER

BLACK
DARK BROWN
MAHOGANY
DRICK
DARK AMBER
AMBER
GOLD
STRAW
CLEAR

FLAVOR WHEEL

BALANCE, FINISH, BODY, PEATY / SMOKY, SHARP / ACIDIC, ASTRINGENT, ROASTED / WOODY, MOLASSES, SWEET / CANDIED, SPICES, HERBAL / VEGETAL, DRIED FRUIT, CITRUS FRUIT, DARK FRUIT, FRESH FRUIT, HEAT / ABM ____ %

FLAVOR NOTES

SMELL / SCENT NOTES

OTHER NOTES

RUM LOG

RUM NAME		DATE TASTED

PRODUCER	DISTILLERY

TYPE / GRADE	COUNTRY OF ORIGIN

STILL TYPE	REGION

AGE	ALCOHOL %	PRICE	BOTTLE SIZE

QUALITY RATING

1	2	3	4	5	6	7	8	9	10

VALUE FOR MONEY

1	2	3	4	5	6	7	8	9	10

COLOR METER

- BLACK
- DARK BROWN
- MAHOGANY
- BRICK
- DARK AMBER
- AMBER
- GOLD
- STRAW
- CLEAR

FLAVOR WHEEL

BALANCE — HEAT / ABM _____ %

FINISH
FRESH FRUIT
BODY
DARK FRUIT
PEATY / SMOKY
CITRUS FRUIT
SHARP / ACIDIC
DRIED FRUIT
ASTRINGENT
HERBAL / VEGETAL
ROASTED / WOODY
SPICES
MOLASSES
SWEET / CANDIED

FLAVOR NOTES

SMELL / SCENT NOTES

OTHER NOTES

RUM NAME		DATE TASTED
PRODUCER	DISTILLERY	
TYPE / GRADE	COUNTRY OF ORIGIN	
STILL TYPE	REGION	

AGE	ALCOHOL %	PRICE	BOTTLE SIZE

QUALITY RATING

1	2	3	4	5	6	7	8	9	10

VALUE FOR MONEY

1	2	3	4	5	6	7	8	9	10

COLOR METER

- BLACK
- DARK BROWN
- MAHOGANY
- BRICK
- DARK AMBER
- AMBER
- GOLD
- STRAW
- CLEAR

FLAVOR WHEEL

HEAT / ABM _____ %

BALANCE, FINISH, BODY, PEATY / SMOKY, SHARP / ACIDIC, ASTRINGENT, ROASTED / WOODY, MOLASSES, SWEET / CANDIED, SPICES, HERBAL / VEGETAL, DRIED FRUIT, CITRUS FRUIT, DARK FRUIT, FRESH FRUIT

FLAVOR NOTES

SMELL / SCENT NOTES

OTHER NOTES

RUM LOG

RUM NAME		DATE TASTED

PRODUCER	DISTILLERY

TYPE / GRADE	COUNTRY OF ORIGIN

STILL TYPE	REGION

AGE	ALCOHOL %	PRICE	BOTTLE SIZE

QUALITY RATING

1	2	3	4	5	6	7	8	9	10

VALUE FOR MONEY

1	2	3	4	5	6	7	8	9	10

COLOR METER

- BLACK
- DARK BROWN
- MAHOGANY
- BRICK
- DARK AMBER
- AMBER
- GOLD
- STRAW
- CLEAR

FLAVOR WHEEL

HEAT / ABM _____ %

BALANCE
FINISH
BODY
PEATY / SMOKY
SHARP / ACIDIC
ASTRINGENT
ROASTED / WOODY
MOLASSES
SWEET / CANDIED
SPICES
HERBAL / VEGETAL
DRIED FRUIT
CITRUS FRUIT
DARK FRUIT
FRESH FRUIT

FLAVOR NOTES

SMELL / SCENT NOTES

OTHER NOTES

RUM NAME		DATE TASTED

PRODUCER	DISTILLERY

TYPE / GRADE	COUNTRY OF ORIGIN

STILL TYPE	REGION

AGE	ALCOHOL %	PRICE	BOTTLE SIZE

QUALITY RATING

1	2	3	4	5	6	7	8	9	10

VALUE FOR MONEY

1	2	3	4	5	6	7	8	9	10

COLOR METER

- BLACK
- DARK BROWN
- MAHOGANY
- BRICK
- DARK AMBER
- AMBER
- GOLD
- STRAW
- CLEAR

FLAVOR WHEEL

BALANCE · HEAT / ABM _____ %
FINISH
BODY
PEATY / SMOKY
SHARP / ACIDIC
ASTRINGENT
ROASTED / WOODY
MOLASSES
SWEET / CANDIED
SPICES
HERBAL / VEGETAL
DRIED FRUIT
CITRUS FRUIT
DARK FRUIT
FRESH FRUIT

FLAVOR NOTES

SMELL / SCENT NOTES

OTHER NOTES

RUM NAME		DATE TASTED

PRODUCER	DISTILLERY

TYPE / GRADE	COUNTRY OF ORIGIN

STILL TYPE	REGION

AGE	ALCOHOL %	PRICE	BOTTLE SIZE

QUALITY RATING

1	2	3	4	5	6	7	8	9	10

VALUE FOR MONEY

1	2	3	4	5	6	7	8	9	10

COLOR METER

- BLACK
- DARK BROWN
- MAHOGANY
- BRICK
- DARK AMBER
- AMBER
- GOLD
- STRAW
- CLEAR

FLAVOR WHEEL

HEAT / ABM _____ %

BALANCE · FINISH · BODY · PEATY / SMOKY · SHARP / ACIDIC · ASTRINGENT · ROASTED / WOODY · MOLASSES · SWEET / CANDIED · SPICES · HERBAL / VEGETAL · DRIED FRUIT · CITRUS FRUIT · DARK FRUIT · FRESH FRUIT

FLAVOR NOTES

SMELL / SCENT NOTES

OTHER NOTES

RUM NAME		DATE TASTED

PRODUCER	DISTILLERY

TYPE / GRADE	COUNTRY OF ORIGIN

STILL TYPE	REGION

AGE	ALCOHOL %	PRICE	BOTTLE SIZE

QUALITY RATING

1	2	3	4	5	6	7	8	9	10

VALUE FOR MONEY

1	2	3	4	5	6	7	8	9	10

COLOR METER

BLACK
DARK BROWN
MAHOGANY
BRICK
DARK AMBER
AMBER
GOLD
STRAW
CLEAR

FLAVOR WHEEL

BALANCE, HEAT / ABM _____ %, FINISH, FRESH FRUIT, BODY, DARK FRUIT, PEATY / SMOKY, CITRUS FRUIT, SHARP / ACIDIC, DRIED FRUIT, ASTRINGENT, HERBAL / VEGETAL, ROASTED / WOODY, SPICES, MOLASSES, SWEET / CANDIED

FLAVOR NOTES

SMELL / SCENT NOTES

OTHER NOTES

RUM LOG

RUM NAME		DATE TASTED

PRODUCER	DISTILLERY

TYPE / GRADE	COUNTRY OF ORIGIN

STILL TYPE	REGION

AGE	ALCOHOL %	PRICE	BOTTLE SIZE

QUALITY RATING

1	2	3	4	5	6	7	8	9	10

VALUE FOR MONEY

1	2	3	4	5	6	7	8	9	10

COLOR METER

- BLACK
- DARK BROWN
- MAHOGANY
- BRICK
- DARK AMBER
- AMBER
- GOLD
- STRAW
- CLEAR

FLAVOR WHEEL

HEAT / ABM _____ %

BALANCE, FINISH, BODY, PEATY / SMOKY, SHARP / ACIDIC, ASTRINGENT, ROASTED / WOODY, MOLASSES, SWEET / CANDIED, SPICES, HERBAL / VEGETAL, DRIED FRUIT, CITRUS FRUIT, DARK FRUIT, FRESH FRUIT

FLAVOR NOTES

SMELL / SCENT NOTES

OTHER NOTES

RUM NAME		DATE TASTED

PRODUCER	DISTILLERY

TYPE / GRADE	COUNTRY OF ORIGIN

STILL TYPE	REGION

AGE	ALCOHOL %	PRICE	BOTTLE SIZE

QUALITY RATING

1	2	3	4	5	6	7	8	9	10

VALUE FOR MONEY

1	2	3	4	5	6	7	8	9	10

COLOR METER

- BLACK
- DARK BROWN
- MAHOGANY
- BRICK
- DARK AMBER
- AMBER
- GOLD
- STRAW
- CLEAR

FLAVOR WHEEL

HEAT / ABM _____ %

BALANCE, FINISH, BODY, PEATY / SMOKY, SHARP / ACIDIC, ASTRINGENT, ROASTED / WOODY, MOLASSES, SWEET / CANDIED, SPICES, HERBAL / VEGETAL, DRIED FRUIT, CITRUS FRUIT, DARK FRUIT, FRESH FRUIT

FLAVOR NOTES

SMELL / SCENT NOTES

OTHER NOTES

RUM LOG

RUM NAME		DATE TASTED
PRODUCER	DISTILLERY	
TYPE / GRADE	COUNTRY OF ORIGIN	
STILL TYPE	REGION	

AGE	ALCOHOL %	PRICE	BOTTLE SIZE

QUALITY RATING	VALUE FOR MONEY

1	2	3	4	5	6	7	8	9	10	1	2	3	4	5	6	7	8	9	10

COLOR METER

- BLACK
- DARK BROWN
- MAHOGANY
- BRICK
- DARK AMBER
- AMBER
- GOLD
- STRAW
- CLEAR

FLAVOR WHEEL

HEAT / ABM _____ %

BALANCE • FINISH • BODY • PEATY / SMOKY • SHARP / ACIDIC • ASTRINGENT • ROASTED / WOODY • MOLASSES • SWEET / CANDIED • SPICES • HERBAL / VEGETAL • DRIED FRUIT • CITRUS FRUIT • DARK FRUIT • FRESH FRUIT

FLAVOR NOTES

SMELL / SCENT NOTES

OTHER NOTES

RUM NAME		DATE TASTED

PRODUCER	DISTILLERY

TYPE / GRADE	COUNTRY OF ORIGIN

STILL TYPE	REGION

AGE	ALCOHOL %	PRICE	BOTTLE SIZE

QUALITY RATING

1	2	3	4	5	6	7	8	9	10

VALUE FOR MONEY

1	2	3	4	5	6	7	8	9	10

COLOR METER

BLACK
DARK BROWN
MAHOGANY
BRICK
DARK AMBER
AMBER
GOLD
STRAW
CLEAR

FLAVOR WHEEL

HEAT / ABM _____ %
BALANCE
FINISH
BODY
PEATY / SMOKY
SHARP / ACIDIC
ASTRINGENT
ROASTED / WOODY
MOLASSES
SWEET / CANDIED
SPICES
HERBAL / VEGETAL
DRIED FRUIT
CITRUS FRUIT
DARK FRUIT
FRESH FRUIT

FLAVOR NOTES

SMELL / SCENT NOTES	OTHER NOTES

RUM LOG

RUM NAME		DATE TASTED
PRODUCER		**DISTILLERY**
TYPE / GRADE		**COUNTRY OF ORIGIN**
STILL TYPE		**REGION**

AGE	ALCOHOL %	PRICE	BOTTLE SIZE

QUALITY RATING

1	2	3	4	5	6	7	8	9	10

VALUE FOR MONEY

1	2	3	4	5	6	7	8	9	10

COLOR METER

- BLACK
- DARK BROWN
- MAHOGANY
- BRICK
- DARK AMBER
- AMBER
- GOLD
- STRAW
- CLEAR

FLAVOR WHEEL

HEAT / ABM _____ %

BALANCE
FINISH
BODY
PEATY / SMOKY
SHARP / ACIDIC
ASTRINGENT
ROASTED / WOODY
MOLASSES
SWEET / CANDIED
SPICES
HERBAL / VEGETAL
DRIED FRUIT
CITRUS FRUIT
DARK FRUIT
FRESH FRUIT

FLAVOR NOTES

SMELL / SCENT NOTES

OTHER NOTES

RUM NAME		DATE TASTED

PRODUCER	DISTILLERY

TYPE / GRADE	COUNTRY OF ORIGIN

STILL TYPE	REGION

AGE	ALCOHOL %	PRICE	BOTTLE SIZE

QUALITY RATING

1	2	3	4	5	6	7	8	9	10

VALUE FOR MONEY

1	2	3	4	5	6	7	8	9	10

COLOR METER

- BLACK
- DARK BROWN
- MAHOGANY
- BRICK
- DARK AMBER
- AMBER
- GOLD
- STRAW
- CLEAR

FLAVOR WHEEL

BALANCE, HEAT / ABM _____ %, FINISH, FRESH FRUIT, BODY, DARK FRUIT, PEATY / SMOKY, CITRUS FRUIT, SHARP / ACIDIC, DRIED FRUIT, ASTRINGENT, HERBAL / VEGETAL, ROASTED / WOODY, SPICES, MOLASSES, SWEET / CANDIED

FLAVOR NOTES

SMELL / SCENT NOTES

OTHER NOTES

RUM LOG

RUM NAME	DATE TASTED

PRODUCER	DISTILLERY

TYPE / GRADE	COUNTRY OF ORIGIN

STILL TYPE	REGION

AGE	ALCOHOL %	PRICE	BOTTLE SIZE

QUALITY RATING

1	2	3	4	5	6	7	8	9	10

VALUE FOR MONEY

1	2	3	4	5	6	7	8	9	10

COLOR METER

- BLACK
- DARK BROWN
- MAHOGANY
- BRICK
- DARK AMBER
- AMBER
- GOLD
- STRAW
- CLEAR

FLAVOR WHEEL

HEAT / ABM _____ %

BALANCE
FINISH
BODY
PEATY / SMOKY
SHARP / ACIDIC
ASTRINGENT
ROASTED / WOODY
MOLASSES
SWEET / CANDIED
SPICES
HERBAL / VEGETAL
DRIED FRUIT
CITRUS FRUIT
DARK FRUIT
FRESH FRUIT

FLAVOR NOTES

SMELL / SCENT NOTES

OTHER NOTES

RUM NAME		DATE TASTED

PRODUCER	DISTILLERY

TYPE / GRADE	COUNTRY OF ORIGIN

STILL TYPE	REGION

AGE	ALCOHOL %	PRICE	BOTTLE SIZE

QUALITY RATING

1	2	3	4	5	6	7	8	9	10

VALUE FOR MONEY

1	2	3	4	5	6	7	8	9	10

COLOR METER

BLACK
DARK BROWN
MAHOGANY
BRICK
DARK AMBER
AMBER
GOLD
STRAW
CLEAR

FLAVOR WHEEL

HEAT / ABM _____ %
BALANCE, FINISH, BODY, PEATY / SMOKY, SHARP / ACIDIC, ASTRINGENT, ROASTED / WOODY, MOLASSES, SWEET / CANDIED, SPICES, HERBAL / VEGETAL, DRIED FRUIT, CITRUS FRUIT, DARK FRUIT, FRESH FRUIT

FLAVOR NOTES

SMELL / SCENT NOTES

OTHER NOTES

RUM LOG

RUM NAME	DATE TASTED

PRODUCER	DISTILLERY

TYPE / GRADE	COUNTRY OF ORIGIN

STILL TYPE	REGION

AGE	ALCOHOL %	PRICE	BOTTLE SIZE

QUALITY RATING

1	2	3	4	5	6	7	8	9	10

VALUE FOR MONEY

1	2	3	4	5	6	7	8	9	10

COLOR METER

- BLACK
- DARK BROWN
- MAHOGANY
- BRICK
- DARK AMBER
- AMBER
- GOLD
- STRAW
- CLEAR

FLAVOR WHEEL

BALANCE
FINISH
BODY
PEATY / SMOKY
SHARP / ACIDIC
ASTRINGENT
ROASTED / WOODY
MOLASSES
SWEET / CANDIED
SPICES
HERBAL / VEGETAL
DRIED FRUIT
CITRUS FRUIT
DARK FRUIT
FRESH FRUIT
HEAT / ABM _____ %

FLAVOR NOTES

SMELL / SCENT NOTES	OTHER NOTES

RUM NAME		DATE TASTED

PRODUCER	DISTILLERY

TYPE / GRADE	COUNTRY OF ORIGIN

STILL TYPE	REGION

AGE	ALCOHOL %	PRICE	BOTTLE SIZE

QUALITY RATING

1	2	3	4	5	6	7	8	9	10

VALUE FOR MONEY

1	2	3	4	5	6	7	8	9	10

COLOR METER

- BLACK
- DARK BROWN
- MAHOGANY
- BRICK
- DARK AMBER
- AMBER
- GOLD
- STRAW
- CLEAR

FLAVOR WHEEL

BALANCE — HEAT / ABM _____ %

FINISH, BODY, PEATY / SMOKY, SHARP / ACIDIC, ASTRINGENT, ROASTED / WOODY, MOLASSES, SWEET / CANDIED, SPICES, HERBAL / VEGETAL, DRIED FRUIT, CITRUS FRUIT, DARK FRUIT, FRESH FRUIT

FLAVOR NOTES

SMELL / SCENT NOTES

OTHER NOTES

RUM LOG

RUM NAME		DATE TASTED

PRODUCER	DISTILLERY

TYPE / GRADE	COUNTRY OF ORIGIN

STILL TYPE	REGION

AGE	ALCOHOL %	PRICE	BOTTLE SIZE

QUALITY RATING

1	2	3	4	5	6	7	8	9	10

VALUE FOR MONEY

1	2	3	4	5	6	7	8	9	10

COLOR METER

- BLACK
- DARK BROWN
- MAHOGANY
- BRICK
- DARK AMBER
- AMBER
- GOLD
- STRAW
- CLEAR

FLAVOR WHEEL

HEAT / ABM _____ %

BALANCE
FINISH
BODY
PEATY / SMOKY
SHARP / ACIDIC
ASTRINGENT
ROASTED / WOODY
MOLASSES
SWEET / CANDIED
SPICES
HERBAL / VEGETAL
DRIED FRUIT
CITRUS FRUIT
DARK FRUIT
FRESH FRUIT

FLAVOR NOTES

SMELL / SCENT NOTES

OTHER NOTES

RUM NAME		DATE TASTED

PRODUCER	DISTILLERY

TYPE / GRADE	COUNTRY OF ORIGIN

STILL TYPE	REGION

AGE	ALCOHOL %	PRICE	BOTTLE SIZE

QUALITY RATING

1	2	3	4	5	6	7	8	9	10

VALUE FOR MONEY

1	2	3	4	5	6	7	8	9	10

COLOR METER

- BLACK
- DARK BROWN
- MAHOGANY
- BRICK
- DARK AMBER
- AMBER
- GOLD
- STRAW
- CLEAR

FLAVOR WHEEL

HEAT / ABM ____ %

BALANCE, FINISH, BODY, PEATY / SMOKY, SHARP / ACIDIC, ASTRINGENT, ROASTED / WOODY, MOLASSES, SWEET / CANDIED, SPICES, HERBAL / VEGETAL, DRIED FRUIT, CITRUS FRUIT, DARK FRUIT, FRESH FRUIT

FLAVOR NOTES

SMELL / SCENT NOTES

OTHER NOTES

RUM LOG

RUM NAME	DATE TASTED

PRODUCER	DISTILLERY

TYPE / GRADE	COUNTRY OF ORIGIN

STILL TYPE	REGION

AGE	ALCOHOL %	PRICE	BOTTLE SIZE

QUALITY RATING

1	2	3	4	5	6	7	8	9	10

VALUE FOR MONEY

1	2	3	4	5	6	7	8	9	10

COLOR METER

- BLACK
- DARK BROWN
- MAHOGANY
- BRICK
- DARK AMBER
- AMBER
- GOLD
- STRAW
- CLEAR

FLAVOR WHEEL

HEAT / ABM _____ %

BALANCE
FINISH
BODY
PEATY / SMOKY
SHARP / ACIDIC
ASTRINGENT
ROASTED / WOODY
MOLASSES
SWEET / CANDIED
SPICES
HERBAL / VEGETAL
DRIED FRUIT
CITRUS FRUIT
DARK FRUIT
FRESH FRUIT

FLAVOR NOTES

SMELL / SCENT NOTES

OTHER NOTES

RUM NAME	DATE TASTED

PRODUCER	DISTILLERY

TYPE / GRADE	COUNTRY OF ORIGIN

STILL TYPE	REGION

AGE	ALCOHOL %	PRICE	BOTTLE SIZE

QUALITY RATING

1	2	3	4	5	6	7	8	9	10

VALUE FOR MONEY

1	2	3	4	5	6	7	8	9	10

COLOR METER

- BLACK
- DARK BROWN
- MAHOGANY
- BRICK
- DARK AMBER
- AMBER
- GOLD
- STRAW
- CLEAR

FLAVOR WHEEL

BALANCE | HEAT / ABM _____ %
FINISH
BODY
FRESH FRUIT
PEATY / SMOKY
DARK FRUIT
SHARP / ACIDIC
CITRUS FRUIT
ASTRINGENT
DRIED FRUIT
ROASTED / WOODY
HERBAL / VEGETAL
MOLASSES
SPICES
SWEET / CANDIED

FLAVOR NOTES

SMELL / SCENT NOTES

OTHER NOTES

RUM LOG

RUM NAME	DATE TASTED

PRODUCER	DISTILLERY

TYPE / GRADE	COUNTRY OF ORIGIN

STILL TYPE	REGION

AGE	ALCOHOL %	PRICE	BOTTLE SIZE

QUALITY RATING

1	2	3	4	5	6	7	8	9	10

VALUE FOR MONEY

1	2	3	4	5	6	7	8	9	10

COLOR METER

- BLACK
- DARK BROWN
- MAHOGANY
- BRICK
- DARK AMBER
- AMBER
- GOLD
- STRAW
- CLEAR

FLAVOR WHEEL

BALANCE
HEAT / ABM _____ %
FINISH
FRESH FRUIT
BODY
PEATY / SMOKY
DARK FRUIT
SHARP / ACIDIC
CITRUS FRUIT
ASTRINGENT
DRIED FRUIT
ROASTED / WOODY
HERBAL / VEGETAL
MOLASSES
SPICES
SWEET / CANDIED

FLAVOR NOTES

SMELL / SCENT NOTES

OTHER NOTES

RUM NAME		DATE TASTED

PRODUCER	DISTILLERY

TYPE / GRADE	COUNTRY OF ORIGIN

STILL TYPE	REGION

AGE	ALCOHOL %	PRICE	BOTTLE SIZE

QUALITY RATING

1	2	3	4	5	6	7	8	9	10

VALUE FOR MONEY

1	2	3	4	5	6	7	8	9	10

COLOR METER

- BLACK
- DARK BROWN
- MAHOGANY
- BRICK
- DARK AMBER
- AMBER
- GOLD
- STRAW
- CLEAR

FLAVOR WHEEL

HEAT / ABM _____ %

BALANCE
FINISH
BODY
PEATY / SMOKY
SHARP / ACIDIC
ASTRINGENT
ROASTED / WOODY
MOLASSES
SWEET / CANDIED
SPICES
HERBAL / VEGETAL
DRIED FRUIT
CITRUS FRUIT
DARK FRUIT
FRESH FRUIT

FLAVOR NOTES

SMELL / SCENT NOTES

OTHER NOTES

RUM LOG

RUM NAME		DATE TASTED

PRODUCER	DISTILLERY

TYPE / GRADE	COUNTRY OF ORIGIN

STILL TYPE	REGION

AGE	ALCOHOL %	PRICE	BOTTLE SIZE

QUALITY RATING

1	2	3	4	5	6	7	8	9	10

VALUE FOR MONEY

1	2	3	4	5	6	7	8	9	10

COLOR METER

- BLACK
- DARK BROWN
- MAHOGANY
- BRICK
- DARK AMBER
- AMBER
- GOLD
- STRAW
- CLEAR

FLAVOR WHEEL

BALANCE
FINISH
BODY
PEATY / SMOKY
SHARP / ACIDIC
ASTRINGENT
ROASTED / WOODY
MOLASSES
SWEET / CANDIED
SPICES
HERBAL / VEGETAL
DRIED FRUIT
CITRUS FRUIT
DARK FRUIT
FRESH FRUIT
HEAT / ABM _____ %

FLAVOR NOTES

SMELL / SCENT NOTES

OTHER NOTES

92

RUM NAME		DATE TASTED

PRODUCER	DISTILLERY

TYPE / GRADE	COUNTRY OF ORIGIN

STILL TYPE	REGION

AGE	ALCOHOL %	PRICE	BOTTLE SIZE

QUALITY RATING

1	2	3	4	5	6	7	8	9	10

VALUE FOR MONEY

1	2	3	4	5	6	7	8	9	10

COLOR METER

BLACK
DARK BROWN
MAHOGANY
BRICK
DARK AMBER
AMBER
GOLD
STRAW
CLEAR

FLAVOR WHEEL

HEAT / ABM _____ %
BALANCE
FINISH
FRESH FRUIT
BODY
PEATY / SMOKY
DARK FRUIT
SHARP / ACIDIC
CITRUS FRUIT
ASTRINGENT
DRIED FRUIT
ROASTED / WOODY
HERBAL / VEGETAL
MOLASSES
SPICES
SWEET / CANDIED

FLAVOR NOTES

SMELL / SCENT NOTES	OTHER NOTES

RUM LOG

RUM NAME	DATE TASTED

PRODUCER	DISTILLERY

TYPE / GRADE	COUNTRY OF ORIGIN

STILL TYPE	REGION

AGE	ALCOHOL %	PRICE	BOTTLE SIZE

QUALITY RATING

1	2	3	4	5	6	7	8	9	10

VALUE FOR MONEY

1	2	3	4	5	6	7	8	9	10

COLOR METER

- BLACK
- DARK BROWN
- MAHOGANY
- BRICK
- DARK AMBER
- AMBER
- GOLD
- STRAW
- CLEAR

FLAVOR WHEEL

BALANCE
FINISH
BODY
PEATY / SMOKY
SHARP / ACIDIC
ASTRINGENT
ROASTED / WOODY
MOLASSES
SWEET / CANDIED
SPICES
HERBAL / VEGETAL
DRIED FRUIT
CITRUS FRUIT
DARK FRUIT
FRESH FRUIT
HEAT / ABM _____ %

FLAVOR NOTES

SMELL / SCENT NOTES

OTHER NOTES

RUM NAME		DATE TASTED

PRODUCER	DISTILLERY

TYPE / GRADE	COUNTRY OF ORIGIN

STILL TYPE	REGION

AGE	ALCOHOL %	PRICE	BOTTLE SIZE

QUALITY RATING

1	2	3	4	5	6	7	8	9	10

VALUE FOR MONEY

1	2	3	4	5	6	7	8	9	10

COLOR METER

- BLACK
- DARK BROWN
- MAHOGANY
- BRICK
- DARK AMBER
- AMBER
- GOLD
- STRAW
- CLEAR

FLAVOR WHEEL

BALANCE · HEAT / ABM ___ % · FINISH · BODY · FRESH FRUIT · PEATY / SMOKY · DARK FRUIT · SHARP / ACIDIC · CITRUS FRUIT · ASTRINGENT · DRIED FRUIT · ROASTED / WOODY · HERBAL / VEGETAL · MOLASSES · SPICES · SWEET / CANDIED

FLAVOR NOTES

SMELL / SCENT NOTES

OTHER NOTES

RUM LOG

RUM NAME	DATE TASTED

PRODUCER	DISTILLERY

TYPE / GRADE	COUNTRY OF ORIGIN

STILL TYPE	REGION

AGE	ALCOHOL %	PRICE	BOTTLE SIZE

QUALITY RATING

1	2	3	4	5	6	7	8	9	10

VALUE FOR MONEY

1	2	3	4	5	6	7	8	9	10

COLOR METER

- BLACK
- DARK BROWN
- MAHOGANY
- BRICK
- DARK AMBER
- AMBER
- GOLD
- STRAW
- CLEAR

FLAVOR WHEEL

HEAT / ABM _____ %

BALANCE, FINISH, BODY, PEATY / SMOKY, SHARP / ACIDIC, ASTRINGENT, ROASTED / WOODY, MOLASSES, SWEET / CANDIED, SPICES, HERBAL / VEGETAL, DRIED FRUIT, CITRUS FRUIT, DARK FRUIT, FRESH FRUIT

FLAVOR NOTES

SMELL / SCENT NOTES

OTHER NOTES

RUM NAME		DATE TASTED

PRODUCER	DISTILLERY

TYPE / GRADE	COUNTRY OF ORIGIN

STILL TYPE	REGION

AGE	ALCOHOL %	PRICE	BOTTLE SIZE

QUALITY RATING

1	2	3	4	5	6	7	8	9	10

VALUE FOR MONEY

1	2	3	4	5	6	7	8	9	10

COLOR METER

BLACK
DARK BROWN
MAHOGANY
BRICK
DARK AMBER
AMBER
GOLD
STRAW
CLEAR

FLAVOR WHEEL

BALANCE, HEAT / ABM ____ %, FINISH, BODY, FRESH FRUIT, PEATY / SMOKY, DARK FRUIT, SHARP / ACIDIC, CITRUS FRUIT, ASTRINGENT, DRIED FRUIT, ROASTED / WOODY, HERBAL / VEGETAL, MOLASSES, SPICES, SWEET / CANDIED

FLAVOR NOTES

SMELL / SCENT NOTES

OTHER NOTES

RUM LOG

RUM NAME		DATE TASTED

PRODUCER	DISTILLERY

TYPE / GRADE	COUNTRY OF ORIGIN

STILL TYPE	REGION

AGE	ALCOHOL %	PRICE	BOTTLE SIZE

QUALITY RATING

1	2	3	4	5	6	7	8	9	10

VALUE FOR MONEY

1	2	3	4	5	6	7	8	9	10

COLOR METER

- BLACK
- DARK BROWN
- MAHOGANY
- BRICK
- DARK AMBER
- AMBER
- GOLD
- STRAW
- CLEAR

FLAVOR WHEEL

HEAT / ABM _____ %

BALANCE, FINISH, BODY, PEATY / SMOKY, SHARP / ACIDIC, ASTRINGENT, ROASTED / WOODY, MOLASSES, SWEET / CANDIED, SPICES, HERBAL / VEGETAL, DRIED FRUIT, CITRUS FRUIT, DARK FRUIT, FRESH FRUIT

FLAVOR NOTES

SMELL / SCENT NOTES

OTHER NOTES

RUM NAME										DATE TASTED

PRODUCER	DISTILLERY

TYPE / GRADE	COUNTRY OF ORIGIN

STILL TYPE	REGION

AGE	ALCOHOL %	PRICE	BOTTLE SIZE

QUALITY RATING

1	2	3	4	5	6	7	8	9	10

VALUE FOR MONEY

1	2	3	4	5	6	7	8	9	10

COLOR METER

BLACK
DARK BROWN
MAHOGANY
BRICK
DARK AMBER
AMBER
GOLD
STRAW
CLEAR

FLAVOR WHEEL

BALANCE, HEAT / ABM ___ %, FINISH, FRESH FRUIT, BODY, PEATY / SMOKY, DARK FRUIT, SHARP / ACIDIC, CITRUS FRUIT, ASTRINGENT, DRIED FRUIT, ROASTED / WOODY, HERBAL / VEGETAL, MOLASSES, SWEET / CANDIED, SPICES

FLAVOR NOTES

SMELL / SCENT NOTES

OTHER NOTES

RUM LOG

RUM NAME	DATE TASTED

PRODUCER	DISTILLERY

TYPE / GRADE	COUNTRY OF ORIGIN

STILL TYPE	REGION

AGE	ALCOHOL %	PRICE	BOTTLE SIZE

QUALITY RATING

1	2	3	4	5	6	7	8	9	10

VALUE FOR MONEY

1	2	3	4	5	6	7	8	9	10

COLOR METER

- BLACK
- DARK BROWN
- MAHOGANY
- BRICK
- DARK AMBER
- AMBER
- GOLD
- STRAW
- CLEAR

FLAVOR WHEEL

HEAT / ABM _____ %

BALANCE, FINISH, BODY, PEATY / SMOKY, SHARP / ACIDIC, ASTRINGENT, ROASTED / WOODY, MOLASSES, SWEET / CANDIED, SPICES, HERBAL / VEGETAL, DRIED FRUIT, CITRUS FRUIT, DARK FRUIT, FRESH FRUIT

FLAVOR NOTES

SMELL / SCENT NOTES

OTHER NOTES

RUM NAME		DATE TASTED

PRODUCER	DISTILLERY

TYPE / GRADE	COUNTRY OF ORIGIN

STILL TYPE	REGION

AGE	ALCOHOL %	PRICE	BOTTLE SIZE

QUALITY RATING

1	2	3	4	5	6	7	8	9	10

VALUE FOR MONEY

1	2	3	4	5	6	7	8	9	10

COLOR METER

BLACK
DARK BROWN
MAHOGANY
BRICK
DARK AMBER
AMBER
GOLD
STRAW
CLEAR

FLAVOR WHEEL

BALANCE, HEAT / ABM ___ %, FINISH, FRESH FRUIT, BODY, DARK FRUIT, PEATY / SMOKY, CITRUS FRUIT, SHARP / ACIDIC, DRIED FRUIT, ASTRINGENT, HERBAL / VEGETAL, ROASTED / WOODY, SPICES, MOLASSES, SWEET / CANDIED

FLAVOR NOTES

SMELL / SCENT NOTES

OTHER NOTES

RUM LOG

RUM NAME		DATE TASTED

PRODUCER	DISTILLERY

TYPE / GRADE	COUNTRY OF ORIGIN

STILL TYPE	REGION

AGE	ALCOHOL %	PRICE	BOTTLE SIZE

QUALITY RATING

1	2	3	4	5	6	7	8	9	10

VALUE FOR MONEY

1	2	3	4	5	6	7	8	9	10

COLOR METER

- BLACK
- DARK BROWN
- MAHOGANY
- BRICK
- DARK AMBER
- AMBER
- GOLD
- STRAW
- CLEAR

FLAVOR WHEEL

HEAT / ABM _____ %

BALANCE
FINISH
BODY
PEATY / SMOKY
SHARP / ACIDIC
ASTRINGENT
ROASTED / WOODY
MOLASSES
SWEET / CANDIED
SPICES
HERBAL / VEGETAL
DRIED FRUIT
CITRUS FRUIT
DARK FRUIT
FRESH FRUIT

FLAVOR NOTES

SMELL / SCENT NOTES

OTHER NOTES

RUM NAME	DATE TASTED

PRODUCER	DISTILLERY

TYPE / GRADE	COUNTRY OF ORIGIN

STILL TYPE	REGION

AGE	ALCOHOL %	PRICE	BOTTLE SIZE

QUALITY RATING

1	2	3	4	5	6	7	8	9	10

VALUE FOR MONEY

1	2	3	4	5	6	7	8	9	10

COLOR METER

- BLACK
- DARK BROWN
- MAHOGANY
- BRICK
- DARK AMBER
- AMBER
- GOLD
- STRAW
- CLEAR

FLAVOR WHEEL

HEAT / ABM _____ %

BALANCE · FINISH · BODY · PEATY / SMOKY · SHARP / ACIDIC · ASTRINGENT · ROASTED / WOODY · MOLASSES · SWEET / CANDIED · SPICES · HERBAL / VEGETAL · DRIED FRUIT · CITRUS FRUIT · DARK FRUIT · FRESH FRUIT

FLAVOR NOTES

SMELL / SCENT NOTES

OTHER NOTES

NOTES

NOTES

NOTES

Made in the USA
Monee, IL
15 October 2020